WHEN THE KIDS ARE HOME FROM SCHOOL

WHEN THE KIDS ARE HOME FROM SCHOOL

CAROL VAN KLOMPENBURG & JOYCE K. ELLIS

BETHANY HOUSE PUBLISHERS
MINNEAPOLIS, MINNESOTA 55438

Parts of Chapter 8 first appeared as "When Does Mom Get a Quiet Time?" by Joyce K. Ellis in the February 1984 issue of *Family Life Today*. Used by permission.

Parts of Chapter 9 first appeared as "Music . . . Freeway to the Heart" by Joyce K. Ellis in the January 1985 issue of *The Bible Newsletter*. Used by permission.

Published by Bethany House Publishers
A Ministry of Bethany Fellowship, Inc.
6820 Auto Club Road, Minneapolis, Minnesota 55438

Printed in the United States of America

Library of Congress Cataloging-in-Publication Data

Van Klompenburg, Carol.
    When the kids are home from school / Carol Van Klompenburg and Joyce K. Ellis.
        p.   cm.

    1. Child rearing—United States.   2. Creative activities and seat work.   3. Family recreation—United States.   4. Child rearing—religious aspects—Christianity.   I. Ellis, Joyce K.   II. Title.
HQ769.V295   1991
649'.51—dc20   91–2348
ISBN 1–55661–159–5   CIP

To the mothers who kept summer journals, completed questionnaires, and answered countless inquiries about the days when their kids were home.
—CVK

To my parents, Ed and Eunice Krohne, who gave me countless memorable summers. To Greg, Sharie, and Maryanne for the fun they've let me have as a mom and for the growth they've inspired through the tough times. And to Steve, who lovingly keeps me on a steady course.
—JKE

CAROL VAN KLOMPENBURG is the author of five books, has published countless articles and poems in periodicals, and has taught college, high school, and preschoolers. She received a B.A. in English from Dordt College and an M.A. in Theatre Arts from the University of Minnesota. For the past ten years she has worked as a free-lance writer and homemaker. She and her husband have three boys and live near Pella, Iowa.

JOYCE K. ELLIS is the author of eight books, including an inspirational book for women, *Plug Into God's Rainbow*, and several books for children and teens. An inspirational speaker for women's groups, she and her husband live in suburban Minneapolis with their three children.

Preface

Coauthoring can be tricky, but with the Bethany staff's loving guidance and prayers, this arrangement has worked rather well. However, because the reader could be confused by individual references or statements either of us may wish to make in the text, we have chosen to identify ourselves by our first names (e.g. Carol remembers . . . or Joyce feels that . . .) and by family designations (e.g. the Van Klompenburgs enjoy . . . or the Ellises have tried . . .).

We believe the two of us bring balance to the book—Carol from the small Iowa town of Pella, and Joyce having been raised in St. Louis, Missouri, and now living with her family in suburban Minneapolis. Carol's children are grade-school age while Joyce's have graduated to their teens, providing her with a different perspective.

Our prayer is that this book will be of help and encouragement to parents everywhere for any time *When the Kids Are Home From School.*

Carol Van Klompenburg
and Joyce K. Ellis

Acknowledgements

It has taken the cooperation of many people to put this book together, and we want to express our gratitude to each one. Thanks to the parents who typed, printed, and scribbled answers to our series of questionnaires about summer parenting or who gave up valuable time, allowing us to interview them. They provided us with over 500 pages jammed with notes about their parenting agonies, ecstasies, and survival tools. We thank the following parents for sharing both their insecurities and their wisdom:

Kathi Armstrong, Ruth Bandstra, Joan Bear, Marilyn Bolkema, Evelyn Charles, Rose Daining, Maryan De Haan, Bonnie Deur, Rosie De Vries, Jean De Waard, Ginger Eskes, Janice Freeland, Judy Godeke, Bette Greidanus, Betti Grevengoed, Kathy Groenenboom, Robin Haack, Cindy Heersink, Lynette Horwath, Jerry and Dianna Jenkins, Tammy Johnson, Betty Kimble, Julane Lamkin, Claire Lynn, Alice Martin, Jane McClain, Betty Miller, Judy and Ted Moser, Judy Oppewall, Carolee Pier, Maureen Rank, Cher Rietema, Linda Schmidt, Beth Schoone-Jongen, Beverly Smid, Carolyn Snow, Esther Stoel, Rachel Te Grotenhuis, Dorothy Ter Horst, Faith Tibe, Kathy Vander Leest, Dot Vander Pol, Kathy Viss, Ona Vititoe, Avis Wagner, Tina Westra, Jeanne Williams, Carolyn Windemuller, Karen Wolthuis, Judie Zwiers.

Special thanks go to Christian bookstore owner Sharon Gosselink for the annotated bibliography of family devotional material in Appendix F.

And may the Lord bless our families for their patience, encouragement, and assistance in helping us meet our deadline.

Joyce would also especially like to thank friends and writing colleagues Alice Bostrom, Lois Holmes, Pam Johnson, and Dorothy Larson for their help, input, and critiques during the preparation of this manuscript. And my endless thanks go to Carol Johnson, who believed in me, and to Charette Barta, who prayed. Blessings!

Contents

Introduction

Each mom is different. Some like hot summers. Some don't. Some find lack of schedule refreshing. Some find it hectic. But we all have one thing in common: In the summer, our kids are home, and that requires adjustments. It brings changes.

Every May, many of us experience mixed emotions about the three months that lie before us. We're eager for summer fun and more time with our youngsters. Sometimes it seems that during the school year we greet them only in passing or catch snatches of conversation while we chauffeur them to school, community, and church activities. So we look forward to getting to know them better. Yet at the same time, we wonder how we will cope when our grade-schoolers descend upon us full time.

How will we keep them busy? How will we handle the extra clutter? How will we settle their seemingly endless squabbling? How will we keep up with the continual demand for meals and snacks? How will we survive traveling to our vacation spot? How will we prevent that deadly infection of boredom?

Often we feel guilty for our reaction. We wonder if other moms have the same feelings. How do they cope?

Surveying moms of grade-schoolers from all over the country—mothers of two and mothers of eight and many in between—we, the authors, have discovered that we are not *alone* in our concerns! Note one mother's graphic response to her feelings as summer approached:

PANIC

Another mom pleaded, "Let's hold off summer for another week! I'm not ready yet."

Through questionnaires and interviews, we learned some of the problems moms feared as they faced extended time home with their kids. But we were also excited about the wonderful, creative ideas mothers devised to handle various situations that arise in their families. We felt like giving them a standing ovation!

This is not a book of 5,496 activities to entertain your children while they are home. It is not a book written by experts to tell mothers how to enjoy flawless, conflict-free summers and holidays. It is a book written by two fellow-strugglers, survivors who wish to pass on the collective wisdom of the many of the mothers (and fathers) we know.

We share Paul's sentiments when he said, "Not that [we] have already obtained all this, or have already been made perfect, but [we] press on . . . toward the goal to win the prize for which God has called [us] heavenward in Christ Jesus" (Philippians 3:12, 14).

And of course much wisdom comes from our mistakes and from learning what *doesn't* work for us.

In this book we want to reach our hands across the table and encourage moms to relax and enjoy the times their kids are home—whether summer or any other time school is out—confident that they have good ideas. There are no absolutely right or wrong ways to parent during these times. We only inhibit our creativity when we worry about "not doing it right."

So, relax and read on. Enjoy. You can do it!

◇ **1** ◇

Those Crazy, Seldom Lazy Days of Summer

M id summer a mom wished aloud, "I want those lazy, hazy, crazy days of summer people sing about."

Her friend replied, "Haven't you heard? They're fiction!"

Most moms have pleasant childhood memories of relaxing summer days in which we primarily did what we wanted to do—no homework to worry about, no teachers to please, no schedules to follow. Play, recreation, and leisure activities filled our blissful hours.

We treasure memories of simple pleasures like hiding in a tree to watch a turtle dove hatch an egg, listening to her coo; curling up in a favorite chair, reading for hours; watching the minnows swirl around in a creek in the woods; making blanket tents over the clothesline in the backyard; or joining siblings in a *Monopoly* game that could last for days.

Myths vs. Reality

As summer approaches, the child in us moms cherishes images of freedom, spontaneity, and endless fun outdoors. In moments of fantasy, we daydream of leisurely days with our children. What we forget is that summer was not like that for our *mothers*!

Soon reality hits. There are still dishes to be washed, floors to be mopped, carpets to be vacuumed, meals to be prepared, clothes to be laundered—the list goes on and on. And it seems that the words *more than usual* could be tacked on to each of these tasks.

Some moms *begin* the summer, expecting it to be "a nice change from the usual rush and demands," as one mother put it. By mid July another mom described her disillusionment: "Summer . . . has been more exhausting and traumatic than I anticipated. I feel even more demands on my time." Other mothers face summer with dread from the start, remembering from previous years how different reality is from their idealized myths.

In addition to our role change and our age, other factors differentiate our childhood summers from those of today. We may have grown up in the country and now find ourselves in suburbia or vice versa. Times have changed as well, and some of the pleasures we enjoyed as children are no longer safe.

One mother from the southwestern United States delighted in her childhood days of playing with brothers and sisters in the desert. "We used to spend whole days out there, taking lunch along," she said. "Mom thought it was great. But I don't dare let my daughter do that. It's not safe without supervision. I hate that. I'd like her to be able to enjoy what I enjoyed."

As we look forward to summer or *any* less structured period (Joyce once "enjoyed" the 24-hour-a-day company of her three grade-schoolers for a 7½-week teacher's strike!), another myth we often believe is that lack of structure means more leisure. A visit from the ghost of summers past should again jolt us back to reality. Even when our time is less structured, we can be extremely busy. How often we get to the end of a hectic day, unable to remember a single thing we accomplished!

So how do we face summer realistically? Perhaps two key words are *acceptance* and *confidence*.

Acceptance

In M. Scott Peck's book *The Road Less Traveled*, he says, "Life is difficult. . . .Once we truly understand and accept [that]—life is no longer difficult."[1]

Having our children home for extended periods of time means they are together more, and they probably will argue more, spill more Kool-Aid, break more irreplaceable objects, and think up countless ways to complicate our lives—however unintentional. That's reality! And if we think all the other moms in our nation are sailing through summer completely organized, enjoying spotless kitchens and children who never fight, we are deluding ourselves. Moms like that don't exist!

It is also good to remind ourselves that, contrary to what we've become used to, there is nothing unnatural about children being at home with their parents. Kids leaving home for school six to eight hours a day, nine months a year, is a relatively recent development in history.

God intended that parents be their children's first and continuing mentors, guides, and friends. But when we are used to the kids being gone all day, it is a shock to our system to have them running around the house, squealing—whether in fear or fun—abandoning wet towels on the newly varnished rocker, or leaving muddy footprints where we just finished mopping.

A woman who was about to take her sixth maternity leave in about eight years was asked if she was going to quit her job this time and stay home with her children. "Are you kidding?" she replied. "I couldn't stand being at home with all those kids all day long." One can't help but wonder why she had them in the first place, but there are days when many of us could empathize with her.

When we can accept the fact that summer—or any time the kids are home—is often hectic, frazzling, and more demanding than when we are home alone, we have half the battle won. Why should we expect anything different?

If we enroll them in lots of activities to keep them out of mischief and develop their interests and talents, our schedule will be hectic—taxiing them around. We can expect that. If we don't send our kids to *any* camps, community programs, or church events, we can expect to hear the familiar words, "I'm bored" more often than if we take advantage of some of these opportunities.

And since none of us has attained absolute sinlessness, there will be many squabbles, misunderstandings, and opportunities to practice forgiveness. Why do we expect total perfection from ourselves—and from our kids, who are still maturing, still so new at learning God's ways?

One mother says, "Sometimes my nine-year-old daughter can be so stubborn that I think she's hopeless. Then fifteen minutes later she'll come to me and say, 'I'm sorry, Mom,' and give me a big hug and a kiss. We both need that."

One of the best things we can do is to pray for extra portions of God's *love* and *grace* to replace our *fears* and our *dread* of the extra work and responsibilities these times bring. "There is no fear in love. But perfect love drives out fear" (1 John 4:18). "And God is able to make all grace abound to you, so that in all things at all times, having all that you need, you will abound in every good work" (2 Corinthians 9:8). "Every good work" includes parenting.

We can also look at summer as an opportunity to have more influence on our kids' lives. Whether our children are in Christian schools or public schools, while they are away from us, they are receiving input from other people, learning what other people think they should learn. When our kids are home, we can look for ways, whether subtle or not so subtle, to impart the values *we* want them to absorb.

Besides accepting the reality of summer and the sufficiency

of God, it also helps to accept the differences in families and in individuals.

Families have unique personalities. The questionnaire responses that spawned this book painted pictures of many different types of families—ones in which schedule and firm discipline were very important and ones in which spontaneity ruled. There were athletic families and more sedentary families; there were those who spent much of their time with neighbors and friends and those who kept more to themselves.

Families also develop their own goals and patterns of working out difficulties based on the collective personalities of the individuals that make up that family.

Comparing our family with other families can be disillusioning. Some free-wheeling moms may feel somewhat less "together" than their friends who have lists for everything—including a master list to keep track of their other lists. Some highly disciplined moms may covet the flexibility of their more easygoing friends. We can often learn from our friends, adopting some of their ways that might work for us, without expecting to be just like them.

Some parents like to give their children a week or so to recuperate from the highly scheduled school-year routine before beginning their summer schedule of chores and activities. Others feel their children need to jump right into the summer agenda. They prepare the kids for it before school is out.

Differences between kids and parents can create stress, too. If a mom and two of her children are laid back while a third child needs a lot of structure, or if another mom and her oldest child are as discipline conscious as drill sergeants while the second child is a dreamer, the friction can heat up a household far more than the rays of the summer sun.

Armed with self-reminders about these differences, however, a parent can accept them and plan ahead, suggesting projects for the structured child to do while the others lounge by the pool, reading, or giving the child-dreamer the freedom to climb a tree and let her mind wander while the others are playing a game.

God made us the way we are. Let's not chafe under the diversity that He, in His infinite wisdom, designed in order to make us all a beautiful mosaic for His glory and enjoyment.

Confidence

A good motto for moms when the kids are home from school is: "In quietness and in confidence shall be your strength" (Isaiah 30:15, KJV). We can't always regulate the quietness of our households as much as we might like, but we can choose to trust God for a quiet spirit within ourselves and find our confidence in Him.

Though supposed experts on child-rearing abound, we believe that the children's parents are the real authorities—on their own children. In her book *Creative, Confident Children*, Maxine Hancock says, "While gratefully acknowledging the insights of the professionals, we need to remind ourselves that from time immemorial, parenthood has been for amateurs—and the amateurs who have done the job best have been those who had confidence that it was their job to do."[2]

Why does God use amateurs to raise children? Perhaps because there are no true experts. Each child is unique, as anyone who has more than one child can attest, and so-called experts can't tell you exactly how to raise a child they have not walked the floor with at 2 A.M. or seen through the crisis of the first day of school.

There are some general principles for good parenting, and we can learn a lot from Scripture and from other parents who have experienced similar situations. But parenting is often a matter of trial and error. Christian moms and dads can take comfort in the fact that the Christ who lives within us will give wisdom as we ask Him and yield control to Him. We can face our daily parenting challenges with confidence.

Even Dr. Haim Ginott, one of the supposed experts, makes an interesting observation about parental confidence in his book *Between Parent and Child*. He writes, "What is the difference between the approach of our grandparents and of ourselves in disciplining children? Whatever grandfather did was done with authority; whatever we do is done with hesitation. Even when in error, grandfather acted with certainty. Even when in the right, we act with doubt."[3]

We don't have to act with doubt or hesitation. We can confidently look forward to the times our children are home from school, knowing that God gives us good ideas and helps us be good parents for our kids. As you read on, sift through the information, ideas, and activities in this book, using what you think might work for your family. The thoughts here may generate other ideas that would work even better for you. But remember, you don't have to do it all! Pick and choose.

Preparing for the Invasion

Some of the women who responded to the summer-moms questionnaire found that simply answering the questions as they arrived at varying intervals throughout the three-month period gave them new insights into their families, their roles, and their own personalities. You may find this helpful, as well.

At the back of the book (Appendix A) there are some questions adapted from the original summer-moms survey. Answering these, whether you write them down or just think about them, can prepare you for having the kids home and help you remain confident throughout that time.

You could, instead, start a separate notebook to give yourself more room to jot down your thoughts. You may find that keeping a summer journal this year can help you face next summer more realistically and hopefully. It may also be a good place to clarify some goals.

Goals? For Summer? Are You Kidding?

At least some of us have that reaction. In spite of what many popular books today suggest, formal goal setting isn't for everyone. The majority of women we surveyed are not formal goal-setting, chart-making moms. In the summer we fly by the seat of our shorts, so to speak. And that's not all bad. Because we operate intuitively out of who we are, our children are often molded in ways we may never know.

But usually, even if we don't write down our goals for when the kids are home or specifically think them through, most of us have ideas of what we want that time to be like.

As Christian parents we would probably say that our ultimate goal is to raise kids who love and serve God, or something to that effect. But under that umbrella, there is room for much variety.

For one mother cleanliness is indeed next to godliness—perhaps only a hair less important. This aspect of her personality shapes her summer goals and schedule. She takes on more of the responsibility for cleaning to assure that it is done to her satisfaction and comfort level. Another mother lowers her standard to increase her family's participation in the shared work load, because participation is more important to her.

In child psychologist Bruno Bettelheim's book *A Good Enough Parent,* he says,

> There is a near-universal bias in our society toward the idea that there is only one right way to do something, while all others are wrong. . . . Parents who rely on "how-to" books for child-rearing have established unconsciously, or more often subconsciously, a parallel between their most intimate personal interactions with their child and the assembly of a piece of machinery.[4]

When we accept the myth that there is only one way to do things, we not only reduce our parenting to machinery assembly and maintenance, but we set ourselves up for unnecessary guilt if we don't "do" our summers (or Christmases or other family activities) like someone else.

Guilt often accompanies talk about goals. Syndicated columnist Dolores Curran surveyed 500 family professionals and assembled a list of the fifteen attributes most characteristic of healthy families. She writes about them in her book *Traits of a Healthy Family.* No family has them all, she readily admits, even about her own. But they are good goals to work toward.

At one gathering where she talked about these traits, a man came to talk to her afterward, feeling rather good about his family. "Four out of fifteen isn't all bad," he said. Curran says, "I laughed and agreed with him, but the woman behind him gasped. Actually, I have more hope for him than for her. A sense of humor is one of the healthy traits. Gasping isn't."[5]

Curran's list would be good to keep in mind or to develop into goals of our own as summer approaches. According to Curran's research, a healthy family:

- communicates and listens
- affirms and supports one another
- fosters table time and conversation
- teaches respect for others
- develops a sense of trust
- has a sense of play and humor
- has a balance of interaction among members
- shares leisure time
- exhibits a sense of shared responsibility
- teaches a sense of right and wrong
- has a strong sense of family in which rituals and traditions abound
- has a shared religious core
- respects the privacy of one another
- values service to others
- admits to and seeks help with problems.

None of these traits or goals conflicts with scriptural principles. On the contrary, they dovetail beautifully with biblical teaching. And how much better to congratulate ourselves for the good progress our family has made, continuing to "press on for the prize," rather than to criticize ourselves for what we haven't attained or to feel inferior to other families because we aren't like them.

Whether the goals we envision are general ones, like those above, or specific ones, involving particular skills or attitudes, we need to ultimately be flexible and leave the results up to God.

Carol remembers that a couple of years ago, she and her boys accomplished half or less of their goals for the summer. But two years later, many of those skills have been mastered. Her boys got there in their own time.

And speaking of leaving the results to God, "You can't *make* your child—God does," says Anne Ortland in *Children Are Wet Cement*, "but you can feed him input."[6]

We as parents can provide opportunity, guidance, and environment, but we are not totally responsible. We cannot make our children what they should be. To think we can is rather egocentric. We can pray and provide help, but only God can put our children together the way He wants them to be.

Same Destination, Different Route

Although we may have goals similar to those of our friends, because of our different personalities we may have different means of achieving those goals. One of Carol's acquaintances has taught her kids to lay out their clothes each evening to save hassles the next morning.

When Carol first heard about this, she felt guilty, disorganized. Then she realized that Kathy is not a morning person, while Carol's metabolism rate drops in half after 8 P.M. But early in the morning Carol is full of energy and can easily help her children choose their outfits for the day. So why should she follow Kathy's pattern? It doesn't fit.

Both mothers had the same goal—children dressed with minimum hassle—but they used different means of achieving it.

Different Roles

Summer is not a cruise ship on which moms are the activity directors solely responsible for keeping children entertained every moment of every day. Sometimes, when we are otherwise occupied, our children can learn to take responsibility for themselves.

A few years ago, when Joyce was pushing a deadline on a children's novel, she explained to her then grade-school-age children, who were used to her typewriter clacking, that she wouldn't be able to play with them all the time or settle minor disputes. She assured them she was available in case they really needed her, but they would have to be responsible for themselves as much as possible so that she could work.

The summer passed quickly despite the inevitable interruptions. Her children amazingly found many projects and activities to occupy their time, and she finished her book by the deadline. But she felt very guilty. In spite of the fact that she rewarded their attempts to occupy themselves, reading them a new chapter of the book every few days, she still felt guilty.

The following summer she cleared her schedule completely, vowing not to take any project that required major writing over the summer. She wanted to devote all of her time to her kids. To her disappointment, they were growing up and had made many of their own plans with friends. They were home far less than previous summers. Another source of guilt.

On one hand, she knows that her book-deadline summer is gone forever. She can never regain that time with her kids. But on the other hand, she knows she did not ignore them completely. She made herself available to take care of genuine needs, and they began to take responsibility for themselves.

We want the times our kids are home to be fun, but we know that if they are going to grow to be mature Christians and useful citizens of the world, they need to begin to take increasing responsibility for what happens in their lives.

As we face the busy days ahead, we may want to remind ourselves of a truth one mom posted on her refrigerator:

Remember—in three months, we'll wonder where the summer went!

Looking Up

Lord,

> *Thank You*
> *for children to love,*
> *for more time to love them,*
> *and for Your love as our model.*

> *Amen.*

◇ 2 ◇

Children, Chores, and Charts

Clutter and dirt seem out of control in many households when the kids are home. If the parents' personalities call for strict order and organization, clutter can cause a great deal of conflict. Regardless of a person's personality type, if friends drop over unannounced, clutter can cause a great deal of embarrassment.

When a Jamaican man from her church visited Joyce at home with her new baby, she apologized profusely for the family's clutter all around them. "What you worry for?" the friend asked. "You're a busy woman, mahn!"

There's comfort in knowing that a certain amount of clutter comes with daily family living. We get so used to seeing other people's houses only when our hosts have cleaned and prepared everything just right for company that we forget that on ordinary days many people have cluttered houses, just like ours.

Still, God is a God of order. We can see it in creation, in the organization of the plant and animal kingdoms, even in the orderly way He preserved each species as the flood was imminent—two by two into the ark.

God is also a creative God, and creativity sometimes requires temporary disorder. The Living Bible says, "When God began creating the heavens and the earth, the earth was at first a shapeless, chaotic mass, with the Spirit of God brooding over the dark vapors" (Genesis 1:1–2). This brings balance. And how good to know that God's Spirit can be present over a chaotic mass— like our family room. (Let's not even think about the dark vapors.)

If we constantly hassle our children over the appearance of the house, we may be sending the wrong signals. Gigi Graham Tchividjian, mother of seven and columnist for *Christian Parenting* magazine, says she has learned to ask, "Which is more important, the muddy footprints or the small feet that made them?"[1]

Mothers tend to find their own comfort level and decide on schedules and chore assignments that help maintain that level of order and cleanliness.

Simple rules like removing shoes when entering the house, cleaning up your own mess, putting away one project before getting something else out, or straightening the house at a specified time each day (e.g. before Dad gets home from work) can be a big help.

As one mom observed her mother-in-law when she came to visit, the older woman's philosophy became obvious: It's just as easy to pick up a toy as to step over it.

However, we know our children need to learn responsibility. And trying to get kids to do their assigned tasks often seems like the biggest chore of all. We dream of some foolproof system that will forever bring a peaceful resolution to the chore war. But for many of us, every system we try—rewards, penalties, charts, and lists—works to some extent for about one to four weeks. Then we may find ourselves resorting to coercion or giving up altogether, wondering if our kids will ever learn.

Why do we bother with chores?

First, because chores are part of being in a family—a way to contribute to the whole—and second, because they are a means of bestowing gifts on our children.

The Parable of the Bangboard

Decades ago, when farmers harvested corn by hand, they attached a bangboard—a long, wide wooden rectangle—to the top of one side of the wagon. Then they walked along the other side and tossed in the corn. The ears hit the vertical bangboard on the far side and fell into the wagon.

The corn resounded loudly when it hit the board, but the board stood firm, and the ears landed in the wagon. Bangboards don't give way. They provide a steady boundary, a wall, a perimeter.

We mothers are bangboards in the enterprise of raising a crop known as the family. When it comes to household chores, our kids may keep hitting that extended side of the wagon, and we may get a little chipped and weatherbeaten. But if we lovingly stand firm, our offspring are less likely to ricochet outside the boundaries we have set. It's all part of living together in a family.

Assigning chores to our children is also a means of giving them three gifts: survival skills, responsibility, and a sense of belonging.

Survival Skills

Sometimes we forget that home skills are not learned by osmosis. Eventually our children will probably live on their own. If they are to know how to clean, cook, do laundry, iron, mend a split seam, or mow the lawn, we need to teach them (or find someone else who can).

Joyce realized quite early that the washing machine was not a complicated piece of machinery, and her children learned to do their own wash as soon as they were tall enough to reach the controls. Her son, by age twelve, took special pride in knowing how to sew on "escapee" buttons, and all three of her children can prepare meals when called upon. The girls have even started their own recipe file boxes.

Some skills seem more glamorous than others. Few kids brag about knowing how to take out the trash, weed the garden, or shovel snow. But they are all part of learning to take responsibility.

In his book *Parents, Take Charge*, family therapist Perry L. Draper reminds us, "The primary motive for giving chores to children is *not* to relieve the parents of work, but to prepare the children for life in the working world ahead of them."[2]

Responsibility

Though we may feel we are showing love for our families by doing all their laundry, cooking, or cleaning, if we do everything for them, they learn nothing. Parents have the privilege of helping children learn the skills necessary to take responsibility for their own needs and the needs of a family once they abandon the nest. And breaks from school are an excellent time to teach some of these skills.

Some moms use an apprentice-for-the-day approach, assigning each child one day a week in which he or she chooses tasks from a list the parents have prepared (washing windows, cleaning the garage, mending clothes, or others appropriate to child's age) and then doing them alongside Mom or Dad. This takes commitment on the part of the parents, but children generally respond better when they're working with someone else. And the parent can give guidance in how to do the job right. This approach also provides one-on-one togetherness time, so important for building self-esteem.

Other parents have children help with the grocery shopping (preferably one at a time), letting them pick out the ingredients needed for a favorite meal the kids will prepare some time that week. This can also help youngsters appreciate the cost of food. And the more our children take responsibility in the daily machinery of running a family, the more secure they feel in their identity.

A Sense of Belonging

When we invite guests to our home for dinner, we don't usually require them to wash the dishes or carry out the trash, but we do expect help with these types of chores from members of our family. Those who live in our household are not guests and should not expect to be treated as such.

Because children *belong* to a family, they can expect to help in some ways with the myriad tasks it takes to keep a family running smoothly. Scripture gives a rather extreme example: "If a man will not work, he shall not eat" (2 Thessalonians 3:10). Most families don't take that literally, but contrary to what our children may believe, it is not cruel and unusual punishment for kids to help around the house. It is quite normal—part of belonging to a family. When all the family members work together as a team, we give each one the gift of feeling needed.

Again, the personalities of the parents often determine the types and amount of work expected from their kids as well as the rigidity of schedules and charts.

Chores Grade-schoolers Can Do

The questionnaire asked mothers how much time their children spend working each day and what tasks are assigned. Daily work times varied, ranging from half an hour to half a day. Tasks differed, but the compilation included nearly every possible household chore. The composite list (see Appendix B) gives new options for chores—everything from setting the table to helping preserve garden produce to organizing toys and games.

One mother admits an ulterior motive in assigning the toys-and-games task: "If the kids sort and organize the toys, they rediscover old favorites and spend time playing with things they had forgotten about."

The list may also provide some ideas of chores we had not considered. For example, Carol had never thought of asking her children to put away their own laundry. It was a task her mother always did. As we read through this list of chores other mothers give their children, we discover that grade-schoolers are capable workers!

Schedules

Some moms have to have structure, so they carefully plan every segment of time throughout the day with chores, play times, devotions, and more. Kathi A., a Michigan mother of six (expecting number seven), posts her summer schedule on the refrigerator. It looks like this:

(Caution: Reading through this schedule may be hazardous to the faint at heart!)

7:00 A.M.   Mom's personal time for devotions and writing.
8:00–8:30   family devotions
8:30–9:00   calisthenics and one-mile jog
9:00–9:15   kids do assigned duties while Mom fixes breakfast
9:15–9:30   eat breakfast
9:30–9:45   breakfast cleanup and other assigned duties for kids
9:45–10:00   clean rooms, make beds, put away pajamas, brush teeth and hair
10:00–12:00 special cleaning project; kids take turns helping Mom
12:00–12:30 prepare lunch
12:30–12:45 eat lunch
12:45–1:00   kids stack dishes, water dog, clear table
1:00–2:00   quiet time
2:00–3:00   swim time
3:00–3:30   snack time
3:30–4:00   yard work, gardening
4:30–5:00   laundry, ironing, sewing, housecleaning
5:00–7:00   free time for kids
5:00–6:00   correspondence and business for Mom
6:00–7:00   prepare dinner with one of the kids, straighten house (duty rotation)
7:00–7:30   eat dinner
7:30–7:45   dishes, clear table, dress the baby, kids feed dog
7:45–8:00   get ready for bed, put away clothes
8:00–8:30   family devotions with Dad
8:30–9:00   sing and rock to sleep
9:00   lights out for younger three
9:30   lights out for older two
9:00–10:00   catch-up time for Mom
10:00–10:30 ready for bed

Indeed, we can tell that Kathi's personality requires structure. (If your schedule is not this detailed, you may want to let your kids see it so they appreciate *your* style. If your schedule *is* this detailed, you may want to let your children see it to prove you're not the only one who makes schedules like this.)

Mothers who are more laid back or spontaneous have simpler but often just as effective schedules *for them.* Many moms expect the children to be up and beds made by 9 or 10 with assigned chores and/or music practice done by lunch time. Then the rest of the day is theirs for play. Some moms don't even care if their children sleep in frequently. As long as the kids are asleep, Mom has some peace and quiet to get things done.

One of the moms in the survey (we'll call her Gloria) became depressed with the idea of schedules. "You ask what our routine is, but we don't have one," she says in embarrassment. "I feed the kids when they are hungry. They are happiest playing what they want, when they want. They don't have assigned jobs, but when the house needs cleaning, we all pitch in."

She continues, "When I talk with other women, I try to hide the truth and give the answers I think I should give. I don't want to tell them that we eat at unscheduled times and that we have no routine. That's too much guilt."

Gloria's husband provides perspective for her, however. He says, "Look at our kids. Are they happy? Are they well? Are they learning? You can see they are. So don't worry about comparisons. Do what works for you."

We suspect that there are more Glorias in the world than Kathis. But both are doing what is right for them. For some of us the challenge of a schedule is to follow routine without being too rigid. For others the challenge is to be flexible without being too wishy-washy. But for all of us the crucial point is not comparison but effectiveness. Is it working fairly well? (No one's schedule works perfectly all the time.) Are we happy and healthy and growing? Then we need not worry or carry around guilt for not doing things exactly like other people do them.

Getting the Chores Done

Mothers are always looking for new ways to motivate their kids to help around the house. Because different personalities respond to different methods, sometimes varied strategies are required. Below are a number of good suggestions shared by the moms surveyed:

- Blitz!—Organize family for a half-hour cleaning blitz—

everybody cleans something, then the family does a fun activity together.

- K.P. assignments—Mark each day of the calendar with children's initials on alternating or rotating days, indicating who has K.P. (Kitchen Patrol) duty.
- Pick-a-job—Every night write out chores for the next day on small slips of paper and place them in a cup or jar. In the morning children take turns drawing chores one at a time until all the chores have been drawn.

  Variation #1: About two days a week, in addition to above, everyone pick a bathroom and clean it or everyone pick a room and dust it.

  Variation #2: If child honestly despises the particular chore drawn, let him or her suggest alternatives. Sometimes kids come up with surprising ideas. (Beware of the child who honestly despises every chore drawn. He may need to learn diversity.)
- Write it down—Write out the chore list and leave it on the table or counter, indicating who is to do what. Often kids prefer reading their instructions rather than hearing Mom tell them what to do. They may also get satisfaction from crossing off each job on the list as they do it. This can work especially well for moms who work outside the home. Children can be expected to have their assigned duties finished by the time Mom gets home.
- The "in-charge" system—Each day the child in charge must: unload the dishwasher, feed and water the dog, set the table.

  Also, the person in charge gets to sit in his favorite TV-watching chair, decides what game the family will play, and decides who sits where in the car.

Probably one of the most effective motivations for kids is having their parents work alongside them. One working mom felt that her biggest problem was getting her ten-year-old daughter to pick up after herself. She decided to work with her daughter in straightening her room before bed each night, which also enabled them to have more time together. Her daughter was happy about the extra attention, and picked up her room much more willingly.

Charts?

Do they work or don't they? Again, it depends on the personality of each mother—and each child. While many parents admit that charts generally work for only a limited time, for some mothers, they are a great organizational tool. For some children they are a great motivational tool. Here are a couple of chart ideas used by the moms surveyed:

Three-ring binder system—Each child has a daily and weekly chore chart kept in a three-ring binder. Child or parent checks off items when done satisfactorily. The example shown is for a thirteen-year-old boy.

Younger children will have fewer responsibilities and tasks more suited to their age. Some parents choose to reward their kids monetarily according to the number of check marks on their charts each week.

One mother using this system says, "After tithing, the money is saved for a family outing—such as a professional baseball game, a water park, adventure park, or an added special event during the family vacation."

Rotating chore wheel—This simple and common chart is made from two circles of cardboard—one at least an inch larger than the other—held together in the middle with a brass fastener. The children's names are written on the inside wheel while chores such as setting table, sweeping kitchen, or doing dishes are written on the outer wheel. The chart is rotated daily. Children police each other, and adults supervise.

Appropriate Assignments

Most mothers make certain that they assign tasks appropriate to the age of the child, but sometimes we become frustrated because we forget that children and chores can be mismatched in other ways.

One mom says, "Katrina does well folding laundry and putting it away, but when Lisa does it, I grow tired of finding my socks and underwear inside out, mismatched, and in the wrong drawers. Lisa is better at unloading and loading the dishwasher and keeping our rabbit happy."

DAILY

S M T W Th F S

Practice piano 30 minutes

Make bed

Pick up bedroom

Load or unload dishwasher

Practice French horn 30 minutes

Read 30 minutes

Keep family room clean

WEEKLY

Do the wash

Fold own clothes

Mow grass

Prepare one meal

Bake one item

Lead mealtime devotions once

Weed assigned area

Other: _____

_____

_____

    Finally, we need to remember that even the best motivating techniques won't make our children into little robots who willingly do everything we ask without hesitation. We wouldn't want that, anyway. People are naturally lazy. Most of us tend to do as little work as we can. Why else are labor-saving devices so popular?

    Carol remembers that each summer she and her three brothers helped her mother preserve summer produce. They peeled bushels of apples while their mother boiled them into apple-

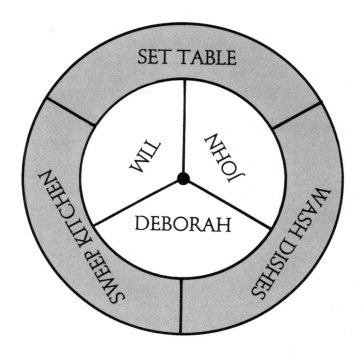

sauce. They snapped beans while their mother blanched them and filled the canning jars. Carol doesn't remember shirking or complaining, but what does her mother remember? Children asking how long until they were done and asking for frequent breaks.

The Light Touch

The mothers surveyed admit that sometimes, when their children don't follow through with their chores and responsibilities, the moms resort to begging, yelling, and making their kids feel guilty. Most of us know, at least in our minds, that humor, positive reminders, and a kind tone of voice are usually far more effective. We just need reminders sometimes.

Joyce's friend Corolee and her husband were foster parents

in a Christian group home to more than seventy children over the years—usually averaging about six to eight at a time. They have now retired, but while Joyce was visiting them in their group home in Tennessee, she noticed that Corolee used a very gentle tone with the children and ended nearly every request or chore reminder with a term of endearment, like honey or sweetheart.

We may not all feel comfortable talking like that, but adding that little touch of kindness at the end of a reminder can completely alter a child's attitude toward the request.

Warnings also help. Saying, "In five minutes I will need you to . . ." cushions the shock and can help kids feel like the request is less of an intrusion on what they're doing at the moment.

Stick to Your Guns!

Surprisingly, quite a few moms said that once they established a routine, they had less trouble getting their kids to do their daily chores. "Once a habit is formed, it seems to stick," one mom said.

Quality is another matter, however. That same mom qualifies her remark: "My sons are prone to working fast and sloppily. The best solution is for me to call them back to task until the job is done right."

Another mom says she also has to carefully check her daughter's work. "That girl would rather kick her underwear under the bed than put it in the hamper," she admits.

A New Jersey mother reports, "I have learned not to feel sorry for my children and do (or redo) their assigned chores. *The task is theirs.* If it is not done well, I send the child back to redo it. This can be trying, but to me it's important that they learn their work must be done well. So each day, I do my chores—and monitor theirs."

While some parents reward jobs well done with treats or cash, others feel that thank yous and compliments are the only necessary rewards. They tell their children, "You are part of this family, and each of us needs to work." Sincere praise can go a long way in helping kids feel good about the work they've done and hopefully make them more willing to help in the future if they know that the work will be appreciated.

A Positive Attitude

We need to be careful not to convey to our kids, either through words or actions, that work is the curse of human beings. Adam and Eve worked, tending the Garden of Eden, *before* they sinned. The curse resulting from their sin was not work itself; it was work with toil, with pain, with sweat, and with thorns and thistles.

A good verse to post on the refrigerator or at the top of a chores chart is: "Whatever your hand finds to do, do it with all your might" (Ecclesiastes 9:10).

————— Looking Up —————

Creator God,
> *help us to be creative*
> *in everything*
> *You call us to do—*
> *even in getting our kids*
> *to bring order*
> *out of their chaos.*

Amen.

◇ **3** ◇

Sibling Quibblings

A rguing, bickering, and fighting can take place at any time in any home. But during the summer or other extended breaks from school, we mothers often feel we can't stand another round of "I did not—You did, too," ping-ponging back and forth. The complaint, "But she hit me back first," puzzles even the sharpest parent.

Most mothers cite quarreling as a major concern when the kids are home. One said, "My mother used to get very upset when we children fought. Now I understand how she felt. I hate conflict and fighting." Another mom said, "If our school ever decides to hold year-round school, I'd schedule my boys' vacations at different times."

Squabbling jangles the nerves, stretches the patience, and violates the conviction deep within us that people who love each other shouldn't fight.

One of Joyce's aunts, a Missouri mother of eight, wrote a column in the *Eureka Times* some years ago about her husband's concern over their children's near-constant squabbles. "Listen to them, Claire," he said. "They hate each other." Claire, who grew up in a large family, provided some perspective for her husband, an only child. "They don't hate each other, Larry," she said. "They love each other. They just don't know it yet."

Today all those children have young families of their own, and Claire's assessment has proven true. There *is* a wonderful spirit of love and cooperation among those brothers and sisters. They readily come to one another's aid in need, and though they live in various parts of the country, they work together on many projects.

One of the boys is now a cardiologist and inventor. His youngest brother, a computer whiz, helped set up a computer system and graphics program that their oldest sister, an artist, uses to design overhead transparencies and promotional material for her inventor-brother's presentations to prospective manufacturers.

It's comforting to know that there is hope!

If we think back to our own childhood, we probably can remember a few spats with our siblings, too. Why do we expect our children to be any different? Sibling battles have been waged since Cain and Abel though not always with such disastrous results.

Sometimes we may wish we could wave a magic wand and eliminate all disagreements among our children. But would we really want to? That's not reality! We do not live in a conflict-free society. People differ in personality, needs, and preferences. Since the home is the training ground for the rest of life, our children need to learn how to work through conflicts with their siblings, with their playmates, *and* with their parents.

During the learning process, the kids are bound to make some wrong moves and falter in some negotiations (as are we), but often we learn more from our failures than from our successes. The problem is that parents understandably get frustrated with loud, tense "negotiation sessions."

Causes

Drs. Don Dinkmeyer and Gary McKay, coauthors of *Raising a Responsible Child*, cite three reasons brothers and sisters quarrel: "Some children fight to gain attention from parents, others to show parents that they can do what they want, even in defiance of their parents' wishes. And some children pick on a favored child to seek revenge on parents."[1]

Certainly some children fight for *all* those reasons and more.

Many Christian books that address the subject of sibling strife offer similar views, but surprisingly, few talk about the role of a person's sinful nature. Perhaps they think of that as a "given."

In addition to the causes above, many disputes—who gets to play with the new *Nintendo* game, who may ride the skateboard first, who can sit in the front seat of the car, who knocked the freshly watered plant onto the freshly vacuumed carpet—stem from plain old ordinary selfishness. When two children both want the same thing at the same time (or want to escape the consequences of some misdeed), they are most likely thinking only about getting what *they* want.

Fatigue and boredom can also be contributing causes.

We know that when we as parents are tired, our defenses are down, we display less tolerance, and we simply don't have the energy to handle irritations the way we would if we were rested. That scenario is even worse for children, who don't have the maturity to know that fatigue can drain their resources for resolving conflict.

Kids may also fight more during the summer because of the element of boredom. We'll discuss boredom more in Chapter 10, but the old saying, "Idle hands are the devil's workshop," certainly applies here.

When Susie is busy building a great new edifice with *Lego* blocks and older brother Charlie has nothing to do, he may decide to commandeer a few blocks to build a marvelous structure of his own—preferably far superior to anything Susie has ever built. The battle lines are drawn, and the first shouts fired. Bullets of blame fly back and forth.

If it's just before dinnertime, neither the kids nor their mother have the energy to work out the situation equitably. Mom, who is up to her wrists in meatloaf mixture, may end up yelling at them, and sending them to watch TV to keep them quiet, solving nothing and leaving a pile of *Legos* for Dad to step over when he comes home from work.

All of the previously cited causes of sibling quibbling can come into play at once. Author Joyce Milburn beautifully sums up all this in her book *Helping Your Children Love Each Other*. She says, "The cause of sibling rivalry in any given family will be a complex patchwork of . . . factors, as individual as the members of that family. For that reason, there are no pat answers. But neither is sibling rivalry an inevitable, hopeless situation from which there is no escape."[2]

Responsibility

We can often get clues for how to deal with certain disputes by understanding what caused them, but sometimes, when we overanalyze motives, we may only be stirring up guilt feelings in ourselves—why have *we* failed in teaching them how to share, how to be kind to one another, how to "get along"?

Why do we take all the blame?

This is another type of responsibility our children need to learn. In addition to learning to take responsibility for work, as discussed in the previous chapter, they also need to take responsibility for their actions.

When we read the story of Cain and Abel, do we blame Adam and Eve and call them failures, or do we hold Cain accountable for killing his brother?

Go back another generation. Even Adam and Eve played the blame game. When God caught them red-handed, Eve blamed the serpent while Adam blamed Eve and even *God* for giving him such an irresponsible wife. God held all three of them accountable and meted out appropriate consequences.

Because we as parents do not have God's omniscience and

often can't sort out who's right or who's at fault, we struggle with how to handle our children's feuds. So *moment by moment* we ask our all-knowing God for wisdom because each situation is different. And parents and children alike get a lot of practice in the art of forgiveness.

When our patience is stretched beyond endurance, we can remind ourselves of how often God has to listen to the squabbling of His children over matters as insignificant as who gets to play with the *Lego* blocks.

Those who are inclined to put Scripture verses in places where their children will see them often (such as the refrigerator), may want to post the familiar: "Be kind and compassionate to one another, forgiving each other, just as in Christ God forgave you" (Ephesians 4:32). It's a good reminder for both children and parents, especially during the "hot" summer months.

Family Climate-control Strategies

Of course we would all prefer to maintain a "cool" family temperature, regardless of the thermometer reading inside or out. And many families head off some of the difficulties that could arise through various means:

Being careful of the example we set—That is, how do we respond to our spouses, relatives, and friends who may at times take advantage of us, insist on their rights, or act thoughtlessly? Few people seem to have even heard of the word *deference*, much less know what it means or practice it. But when two people have opposing viewpoints or desires, often one needs to defer to the other rather than insist on his or her own rights. We can translate this into a common type of sibling debate:

Sammy may have every right to play the piano now, but if Cindy needs quiet to study for a test the next day, Sammy can learn to occupy himself in other ways, waiting until Cindy is through studying before he plays the piano. That's deference. It's another kind of love—acting in the best interest of the other person.

In conflicts with *our* peers, we as parents can model Christian love to our children by allowing the other person's needs or desires to prevail or by working out a compromise. The gentle principle of deference has gotten lost in today's assertiveness quest. But we can dust it off and put it to work as a powerful tool in settling disputes.

Showing love and respect for each member of the family—One of the greatest gifts we can give our children is the understanding that love is more than a noun indicating an emotion. Love is also an action verb. Many times we don't feel loving toward other people, especially when they have done something to irritate or hurt us, but feeling often follows kind actions on another's behalf. When our feelings waiver, our actions can stabilize our love.

We also show respect for our kids by listening to them. There are days, however, when we feel "all listened out." One child chronically complained that people were always interrupting her until her mother reminded her that it was because *she* seldom stopped talking. Respect goes both ways. As we set the example, our *children* need to learn to show respect by listening to others, too.

Speaking well of siblings without implying comparisons—How we talk about our children, whether to their brothers and sisters or to people outside the family, can often set the whole family tone. When one child is complaining about something a sibling did, we can balance the conversation by pointing out some of the offending child's good points. But it's always good to remember that children often see comparisons where we aren't drawing them. Balance is an issue we will forever be dealing with. The tension keeps us on our toes.

Practicing common courtesies such as please, thank you, you're welcome, and I'm sorry—Things like letting another go first in a game, allowing someone else to have the biggest piece of cake, greeting family members when they come home, and phoning to advise of a change in plans show courtesy and respect. These, too, are things we can model for our children.

After-the-fact Strategies

Time and time again, mothers in the survey cried out for help with their kids' daily (hourly?) skirmishes. One mom echoed the line from the old TV commercial: "What's a mother to do?"

When asked how they dealt with the dilemma, they came up with some of the same answers given in most books by the "experts." Either they've been reading the same books, or they intuitively act wisely—probably a little of both.

Again, parents are the real experts on their own children, and through trial and error, we often find what works best for us in different situations. We may just need a little variety from time to time. But we can often gain a better perspective on any method we use if we look at its potential for helping our soon-to-be-adult children solve their own future conflicts.

Though numerous variations can be worked out, in accordance with the personalities of those involved, there are a few common approaches that help parents deal with their own family feuds.

Separate 'em—This was the most frequently cited solution by far. Many moms tell the children to go to separate rooms until they calm down. When tempers have cooled, the kids go to each other and resolve their difficulty. This is a good model for adult conflict resolution. We would all do well to negotiate only after we've cooled down rather than lashing out in the heat of the moment.

One mom asks both parties to think about what *they* did that contributed to the problem. "After a short time I come back and ask them to tell me what they did that they shouldn't have done. . . . How hard it is for them to see their own error sometimes—because they are focusing on the other person's error!" This is a common adult problem, too.

Let 'em fight it out—Some moms and dads follow the advice many "experts" give and let the children fight—but out of the parents' sight and hearing. It is an effective method if the altercation is particularly geared to getting the parents' attention, because if we are ignoring the conflict, there is no reason for the children to continue.

"We really can't solve our children's squabbles by intervening," says psychologist Bruce Narramore. "No matter whom we blame or how we do it, one of the children is rewarded for misbehavior. This increases the likelihood of another fight at a later date."[3]

Let 'em work it out—Some moms make the kids sit across the table from each other (or on two chairs on opposite sides of the room, facing each other) until they can work out a solution and apologize to each other. This can keep the kids occupied for a *long* time. Stubbornness dies hard.

Time out—Time out requires a small portable kitchen timer, a location (a chair in the corner of a room or any other boring place), and a specified amount of time. With the children's input, parents make out a list of undesirable behaviors that warrant a time out: hitting, talking back, lying, quarreling, anything that is especially grievous in their family situation. When one of the behaviors occurs, the child must sit at the time-out location until the timer rings. During time out, the child must not speak or be spoken to.

Parents with hockey fans in their family could call this "penalty-box time"—same principle.

Addressing grievances—Some families use a family meeting held regularly or sporadically (depending on their lifestyle and personalities) to air grievances. At that time all the members of the family have opportunity for input on how to solve the conflict. If children are prone to tattling, they can be told to save it for the family meeting. But sensitive parents will be sure to schedule one as soon as possible to address the issue that's bothering the child.

Other families use a "Tattle Book." Authors Verna Birkey and Jeanette Turnquist describe this technique in their book *A Mother's Problem Solver.* "Instead of running to Mother with petty grievances against each other, we had our children list these in a book. At the end of the week we went over them together. . . . Often, by the time we read the book, these things had become hilarious. . . . It seemed to relieve the pressure of dealing with them when spirits were high."[4]

Humor—If there is any way to help the kids see humor in a situation, do it. We give our children a wonderful gift when we teach them not to take life so seriously. Will it matter in two hundred years who ate the last Toll House cookie or who got to play computer games two minutes longer?

Avoiding Conflict?

We naturally avoid conflict because it's painful and uncomfortable. But just as a fiction plot is dead without conflict, so are our lives. Characters in a novel or short story *grow* through conflict. So can we.

James wrote some encouragement for situations like this, to which we've added a few adaptations in brackets for moms with feuding kids (James 1:2–5):

> Consider it pure joy, [mothers], whenever you face trials of many kinds [with your kids], because you know that the testing of your faith develops perseverance. Perseverance must finish its work so that you [and your children] may be mature and complete, not lacking anything. If any of you lacks wisdom [especially in settling sibling quibblings] [she] should ask God, who gives generously to all without finding fault [as we are prone to do], and it will be given to [her].

That's a tremendous reassurance and promise!

We may not like wearing the "zebra shirt," but there has to be at least one referee in every sport.

If we look at sibling quibblings as teaching opportunities rather than intrusions or something that we shouldn't have to deal with, our time with our kids—spats and all—will be much more positive.

_____ *Looking Up* _____

Lord,

> *When the kids are home*
> *we need*
> > *wisdom*
> > > *patience*
> > > > *and joy*
> *in the midst of*
> > *bickering*
> > > *quarreling*
> > > > *and squabbling.*
> *We draw upon*
> *Your*
> > *infinite*
> > > *resources,*
> *All-sufficient God.*

                                        Amen.

◇ 4 ◇

"What's There to Eat?"

When our kids are home, sometimes it seems we should install a revolving door on the refrigerator. The perpetual cry, "What's there to eat?" can wear us out quicker than a two-mile jog.

Some moms have the type of personality that motivates them to make out menus for the week in advance. Others are more spontaneous and keep many commonly used ingredients on hand so that there are a number of choices for each meal. But most of the mothers in our survey say that meals and snacks are a continual battle. Sometimes it is a battle to get kids to eat and sometimes to get them to stop.

Meal Routines and Planning

Routines vary from household to household, too. A few moms try to prepare every meal. Many fix only a common breakfast and dinner for the family. One mother admits that her family's eating schedule is quite irregular. "The kids get up and eat breakfast at different times. Lunch is usually sandwiches or fast food. We all try to eat together in the evening, even if it is late because of the kids' ball games."

Some mothers post the week's menus for each meal on the

refrigerator. Others let the kids choose and fix their own breakfasts and lunches; then Mom cooks dinner. Some kids take turns with their parents in preparing all meals. Often, the way meals and snacks are handled varies according to the family's schedule that particular day or week.

We applaud the organized mother who truly plans ahead. One wrote, "I plan my menus for the whole week, starting with grocery shopping day. But I don't plan and shop on the same day lest it overwhelm me. (I don't especially enjoy getting groceries.) I write my menus in brief on my calendar and also make note of early preparations necessary (e.g. if I'm planning to serve homemade chili on Thursday, I'll write 'thaw hamburger and soak kidney beans' on Wednesday's date)."

But we also applaud the mother whose personality is more spontaneous, who likes to be creative and truly doesn't know what she'll be in the mood to fix until the time comes.

Mealtime Guilt

Some of the mothers in the survey indicated guilt or frustration at not being more organized in menu planning, getting everyone together for meals, and providing balanced nutrition. Obviously, if we do no planning so that there isn't any food in the house to prepare, and if we never have the whole family together for a meal, and if our version of the four basic food groups is McDonald's, Burger King, Hardee's, and Wendy's, we are in trouble.

But since there is no scripture edict that says, "Thou shalt eat three meals, verily three meals a day only, drawing in perfect harmony from the four basic food groups, yea, verily all being at one table as often as ye gather for a meal," we may assume some measure of grace in this area.

We can find balance in remembering two things: First, we live in a fast-paced society in which there *will be* schedule conflicts; second, mealtime can be a haven, an important time of building and maintaining family unity in our conflict-filled, fast-paced society.

Mealtime Togetherness

It's folly to enroll our kids in summer school, tee-ball, and swimming lessons as well as volunteering our own services for community theater and nursing home visitation while our husband has to work overtime, and then wring our hands because we never have a meal together. Yet mealtime is important. To some families, it is almost sacramental. So, we need to make difficult choices.

One mother who came to this conclusion wrote, "I am eliminating several things from our children's schedules and mine. I have found that if they are tied up with too much 'structure,' their commitments overlap and we never get to see each other *all at the same time.*"

There is something warm and wonderful about eating together—often some of our fondest memories are of dinner dates with intimate friends. The evening meal, especially, is a good time for pouring out the events of the day, validating them and ourselves, sharing exciting news as well as incidents that bothered us. Often the menu is the least important part of the meal because we draw nurture from simply being together. We identify again with the family to which we belong and draw strength from that bond we have as a family and as children of God.

When the kids are complaining about the food and kicking each other under the table, we may have a hard time believing all that. But in ten or twenty years they probably won't remember the kicks under the table as much as the kicks they got out of listening to one another's wild stories and crazy antics.

And so we want to be together for meals as often as possible and manipulate our schedules accordingly, but we gain nothing by beating ourselves over the head because we can't be together for every meal—or even every evening meal. To paraphrase the common first and last lines of many prayers, "We thank you, Lord, for the opportunity we have to be together, and ask you to bless us as we go our separate ways."

Making Mealtime Memorable

Whenever we are together, we parents can look for ways to keep meals fun. One of the basic elements of humor is the element of surprise. Sometimes simply preparing an old favorite in a different way can bring a cheerful spirit to the meal table. Joyce's kids loved her Mickey-Mouse-shaped pancakes (made by pouring two smaller circles of pancake batter to connect to the top of the basic pancake). They now make them themselves. And her son once got into the spirit of "the different" by adding green food coloring to the scrambled eggs. Maybe he was unduly influenced in his early childhood by Dr. Seuss's *Green Eggs and Ham.*

Bonnie, an Iowa mother of three, says that once in a while they have a "fun lunch," such as yogurt and party mix. "It's something unlunch-like but healthy," she says.

Candlelight lunches or suppers make for another popular way of adding life to the ordinary. Carol's kids ask for one every few weeks. She gets out the tablecloth, place mats, and candles, and pulls the drapes to darken the room. By candlelight even pizza or hot dogs can be exciting.

While enjoying elegant or simple fare, animated conversation can also make mealtimes more pleasant. If the kids run out of things to talk about (does that ever happen?), some moms stimulate their kids' imaginations by asking questions such as: If you could go anywhere on vacation, where would you go? Somewhere in our state? Another state? Another country?

Trying new or unusual cuisine also adds variety and fun. Esther, an Indiana mother of four, writes, "Two years ago we researched French cooking. We checked out several books from the library and picked out breakfast, lunch, and supper recipes. When my parents traveled to see us, we fixed all our special recipes for them on our 'French Day.'" This family worked on authentic Mexican menus another year. The possibilities are endless.

Cool-kitchen Strategies

Trying to come up with "something different" all the time isn't easy, especially if you're also trying to keep cool in the summer heat. Most of us avoid using the oven unless absolutely necessary, which limits our tried-and-true recipe selections. And because moms get tired of serving the same things all the time, we asked the women surveyed to send along some of their easy and/or cool-kitchen recipes. (See Appendix C for their selections plus a few favorites from Carol and Joyce.)

There are other strategies many mothers use from time to time, but sometimes we forget about them. Below you will find some reminders about a few of a summer mom's best friends. Pick and choose what you think might work for you.

Microwave—If you have a microwave, use it for more than heating vegetables. It greatly reduces cooking time on any food and doesn't heat up the kitchen. Most conventional recipes can be converted for microwave use. One tip is to find a similar recipe in a microwave cookbook and compare. Follow general directions and work out time conversions from other comparable recipes.

Crockpot—Dust off that crockpot you got for a wedding or anniversary gift. You can begin initial dinner preparations in the morning while the kitchen is cool, and cook throughout the day with little or no tending. Crockpots don't heat up the kitchen, either, and again, many conventional recipes can be converted. While you're dusting off the crockpot, dust off the little recipe booklet that came with it. It's a gold mine for summer cooking. If the recipe booklet has disappeared into the Bermuda Triangle of your kitchen drawers, check out a crockpot cookbook from the library and copy some recipes that look interesting. Even such things as quick breads and puddings can be made in a crockpot. There are also a few crockpot recipes to try in Appendix C.

Outdoor grill—Leave the heat of cooking outside where it will feel at home. Some of the simplest meals can be prepared on the grill—virtually any meat, baked potatoes, and frozen corn or corn on the cob (foil-wrapped over the coals). And what simpler, more fun dessert is there than marshmallows toasted while the coals still have a little life in them?

Older grade-school kids can learn to grill safely, too, and often take pride in doing so. One mom says, "Our son interviewed a chef from a fancy restaurant in town for a project at school, and the man gave him one of the paper chef's hats they wear. Now our son enjoys grilling hamburgers outside, wearing his official chef's hat."

Stove-top cooking—Of course, foods that can be prepared or heated in a skillet or saucepan also keep the kitchen a little cooler than those baked or broiled. We've included a few stove-top recipes in the appendix, too—including one for a pineapple upside-down cake made in an electric skillet!

Make-ahead strategies—Many moms lose energy about the time of day they need it most—time to fix dinner. One mother writes, "I often cook my main supper dish in the morning when it isn't hot. Then late afternoon, I microwave it, or we eat it cold. The kitchen stays cooler, and suppertime preparation is faster." Another mom who uses this approach says, "I've found that if I can get the evening meal prepared earlier in the day, or at least have some preparations done, that part of the day goes much smoother."

Other moms make double or triple batches of a recipe at a time, freezing the extra portions for quick reheating on busier days. One mother does this with submarine sandwiches. "I make a lot of submarine sandwiches at one time with ham, salami, cheddar, and Swiss cheese," she says. "Then I warm them in the microwave when we need a quick meal."

And don't forget, food doesn't have to be hot to be nutritious. A cold supper of two or three kinds of cold salad or one salad and a fruit accompaniment can often be more refreshing than a hot meat-and-potatoes meal. (See Appendix C for some good salad recipes.)

Fatigue

Evie, a mother of five from New Mexico, knows what it means to be fatigued when she picks up her kids from the sitter after work and takes them grocery-shopping with her on the way home. How does she handle it?

"Each kid can pick out a one-dollar meal at the store and fix it at home while I unpack the groceries," she writes. "They get things such as Spaghetti-Os, macaroni and cheese, or frozen mini-pizzas. It makes lots of dirty pans and gets a little crowded around the stove, but the kids think it's fun, and it has been the easiest solution for my frazzled nerves." Other moms might find children crowding around the stove the last "frazzled" straw, but it has worked for her.

Letting the Kids Take Over

Sometimes we experience fatigue because we try to do too much ourselves. As we've discussed in previous chapters, one of our goals as parents is to prepare our children for the day when they will have to live on their own. And cooking is one of those survival skills they'll need to know.

One father was becoming concerned that his daughter was so wrapped up in her music lessons, music practicing, music performances, and listening to music, that she wasn't learning much else. He gave his daughter an assignment the summer before she went into junior high. He said, "You are going to learn to cook this summer. Some day you may want to get married, and a husband can't eat quarter notes." Then he and his wife helped her plan menus, do the shopping, and learn how to follow recipes.

Some may call his attitude archaic, but the fact remains that women still do the majority of the cooking in most families. His point was valid. And he helped his daughter learn everything from comparison-price shopping to using the extra little garnishes that make food attractive as well as nutritious and good tasting.

Both sons and daughters can learn how to cook during their grade-school years. Tomorrow's brides will thank the mothers of today's boys for giving these future husbands the skills necessary to share the work load in the kitchen.

And sharing the work load for preparing meals and snacks can be one of the more fun chores we give our children. It allows them to be creative, gives them pride in accomplishment, and helps them appreciate the cost of food and the work parents do to provide food on a daily (hourly?) basis.

Nutrition

The times when our kids are home on break is a good, more relaxed (sometimes) opportunity to teach them about nutrition.

Most children learn about the four basic food groups (dairy, meat and poultry, bread and cereal, vegetables and fruits) at school, so we can build on that at home, reminding them as they help prepare food or come up with ideas for what to get at the grocery store, that we need a good balance of nutrients to keep our bodies in good condition.

Sometimes parents become preoccupied with nutrition, however, feeling a heavy rain cloud of guilt over their heads if they don't have a properly balanced meal every time they sit down at the table. One mother confided, "I wonder if I should tell anyone that our lunch one day was red licorice and lemonade."

Surely, we wouldn't want a steady diet of licorice and lemonade for our kids, but an occasional "unconventional meal" probably won't doom our children to some heinous incurable disease. They may be healthier in the long run for having had a little fun that day.

We can also teach them the importance of a variety of texture and color on the plate. It's certainly more appealing, for example, to sit down to macaroni and cheese, broccoli, and tomato soup than macaroni and cheese, applesauce and scalloped potatoes.

Food Gripes

Now that we've mentioned broccoli, we might as well discuss the matter of picky eaters. A number of families in our survey admitted that they had some problem with this.

Some parents require children to eat at least a little bit of everything served, trying to avoid serving foods too often that they know their children don't like. On the other hand, Carol's solution for mealtime pickiness is a peanut butter sandwich. If the kids *try* what's being served and don't like it, they may substitute a peanut butter sandwich.

Birkey and Turnquist pass along another mother's solution:

> At dinner time we had the usual gripes about food that various family members didn't like. I was wondering what to do when I received a letter about world hunger and found a small bank. So we started the policy that anyone who makes a face or complains about the food puts a nickel in the bank for hungry children in the world. We have hardly collected enough to do anyone any good. If someone ever looks askance at a dish, another child is sure to say, "Well, that sure looks like a nickel to me."
>
> It has made a lot of difference in the dinner-time atmosphere. We have lots of laughs and willingness to try new dishes. And the bank is filling with willing offerings.[1]

Lunchtime Ideas

Sometimes we wrack our brains for ideas other than cold sandwiches, especially if that is what our kids normally take to school for lunch. Tortillas are a fun alternative to bread. There are a couple of burrito recipes in the appendix, and here are a few more suggestions: Spread a tortilla with thin layers of peanut butter and jelly; then place a whole banana in the middle and roll up. This is a favorite on the kids' menu at a Minneapolis Mexican restaurant. Serve with a glass of milk, and you have balanced nutrition (dairy, protein, bread, and fruit) as well as happy kids.

Children can use their imaginations to come up with other tortilla recipes. (Tortillas aren't just for burritos anymore.)

Pocket bread also offers a different twist to old favorites. A few thin slices of turkey, a little Swiss cheese in a pita (pocket bread) zapped in the microwave (or heated in the oven) until the cheese melts is another quick, nutritious lunch. Or try scrambled eggs with a little sausage or bacon bits in a pita. The variations are endless. Enlist your kids' help in coming up with new ideas. Kids are very creative.

Even a bologna sandwich takes on a fun character when you lightly fry the bologna (no grease needed). If you vent the slice with a one-inch slit in the side (which widens to look like a profile-view mouth as it cooks) and make a little hole for an eye, you can call it a Pac-man sandwich. Joyce's kids like them with catsup and mayonnaise (or Miracle Whip) on the bread.

When parents let their imaginations—and their kids' imaginations—go, they can often think up marvelous new fun foods their family will enjoy.

Snacking Rules and Choices

Many moms who responded to the survey had a common problem—snacking. Most also had this common rule: No snacks within one hour of meals. Other rules cited more than once were: Snacks are allowed only if children finished all of their previous meal, and no eating without asking first.

Some moms schedule regular snack times (e.g. at 10 A.M. and 3 P.M.) and allow snacking at no other time.

Others give free reign but only to certain approved snacks, such as fruit, carrot sticks, or ice pops. Many prohibit or limit the amount of junk food in the house so that it's not available for indiscriminate nibbling. Some parents would prefer to have less snacking; but since one or both spouses enjoy snacking, it's hard to impose rules on their offspring to the contrary.

In order to save repeated opening and closing of the refrigerator door, one mom keeps a styrofoam cooler containing cold drinks and approved snacks in front of the refrigerator.

Recipes for some of the surveyed moms' choices for snacks are included in Appendix C. Many can be prepared by children.

Some moms are concerned about snacking because they had no restrictions as children, which led to a weight problem as they grew older. Snacking can also be frustrating to moms who enjoy cooking and see their children turn up their noses at nutritious food at mealtime because they snacked too recently.

Regardless of whether we have strict rules or more flexible ones, as long as we keep an eye on overall nutrition, our children will likely grow up strong and healthy enough to prepare snacks for their own youngsters.

_____ *Looking Up* _____

Lord,

> *You understand*
> *our desire*
> *to see our children*
> *fed properly.*
> *You were the Master*
> *at making food stretch—*
> *to feed 5,000;*
> *teach us Your compassion*
> *for spirit and body*
> *for Your glory alone.*
>
> *Amen.*

◇ 5 ◇

"While I'm Gone, Remember . . ."

It takes all the running you can do to keep in the same place," the queen told Alice in *Through the Looking Glass*. "If you want to get somewhere else, you must run twice as fast."

The mother who works outside the home or has a number of outside commitments knows the perpetual "winded" feeling of trying to keep pace on the treadmill of day-to-day living.

Louis and Kay Moore, journalists for the *Houston Chronicle* and parents of two children, describe the breathless pace many families keep. "When both spouses work outside the home, they often feel like racehorses covering a vast track in a limited time stretch, as they try to compensate for the absent full-time homemaker in their lives."[1]

The pace is bad enough, but mothers who are employed outside the home also frequently battle with fear and guilt over having to leave their children. Although the phrase, *mothers who work outside the home*, is more cumbersome, we prefer to use it rather than *working mothers*, because we contend that *all* mothers are working mothers. However, neither is this the *best* moniker, because many mothers deal with the two-directional tug of home-based employment. Whether employed or not, nearly every mother knows the uneasiness of leaving her kids home alone.

Absentee Mothering

Even if it's only for an hour or two while we go shopping or run errands, we are concerned about the problems that could arise while we are gone. We jump at the sound of a siren, certain a fire engine is speeding toward our house. We worry about the mischief our kids can get into.

Carol recalls coming home from her part-time hospital job to find her two sons and three neighbor boys engaged in a tennis ball war in the family room. She cringed as the tennis balls thudded into the wood paneling. Although they tried to assuage her anger by showing her that they had carefully removed the pictures from the walls and draped the telephone with a blanket, she was not convinced. She repeated her previous edict that tennis balls were for outside play only and pronounced appropriate consequences.

While some might chalk this incident up to the adage, "boys will be boys," many of the problems that could arise are much more serious. We live in a world of day-care horror stories that evoke intense parental concern.

Working outside the home is a tough decision, but now more than half of the mothers in the U.S. are in some way gainfully employed, inside the home or out. This figure was also reflected in the responses from the women we surveyed. Some worked full time or part time outside the home; some worked varying hours in their own businesses at home. All mothers, regardless of their employment status, were sensitive to the issue of leaving their grade-school kids at home while they were away. Although we will be spending some time discussing the particular dilemmas of mothers who work outside the home, many of the principles mentioned here will apply to all mothers.

Who's Watching the Kids?

Many moms wait to join or rejoin the work force until their children are of school age. However, we need to beware of the attitude that once our kids are in school, they don't need us as much. Former schoolteacher, Mary Beth Moster says,

> We must not listen to those who would say that these

growing-up years are less important just because they represent a lull between the storms of the "twos" and the "teens." Vital things are happening in the children's lives as they are growing, maturing, and becoming more responsible.[2]

Waiting until the kids are all in school eliminates some child-care problems but certainly not all of them. The workday at many jobs is considerably longer than the school day, requiring Mom to leave earlier than the kids and get home later. Summers, holidays, and kids' illnesses cause continual conflicts.

Mothers with younger children usually employ a sitter or leave their children at a day-care or latch-key program when schedules conflict, but illness poses a particular problem.

A Minneapolis woman recently became involved in litigation over just such a conflict. Her employer fired her for excessive absenteeism when her child was chronically ill. She understands that they needed a dependable worker, but she is fighting the denial of unemployment benefits. The mother argues that she tried to find suitable help but was not able to find anyone who would care for her sick child. Day-care centers would not take contagious children, and the expense of in-home day care was prohibitive. She said that one service even refused to let her interview the baby-sitter beforehand.

These unresolved issues are reason enough for many mothers to avoid working outside the home, and some who have tried to straddle both worlds are returning home to plant both feet firmly in the home sphere. Working outside the home isn't for everyone, and there is nothing second rate about being a stay-at-home mother. The decisions are too important to be made lightly. After weighing the options, and much prayer, both husband and wife must be united in their choice according to their understanding of God's will for them.

When a mom does work outside the home and her children are too young to be left alone, there are a variety of choices for day care, depending on the parents' personalities, their children's needs, and their family's lifestyle. Options include calling upon the help of grandparents or other relatives, in-home day care, neighborhood or other organized facilities, such as those provided by corporations or community-sponsored public and private day-care centers.

Those who wish to employ sitters in their own home often seek them out among their relatives, church family, or close friends and neighbors. Churches are a common first avenue to explore. Parents feel that if they choose from among their own congregation, they may be fairly sure of finding people of similar convictions and values.

Teenagers are a common choice for summertime, but many teens can't handle the daily commitment required. One woman solved this problem by hiring two teenaged sisters, who took turns, allowing each to have some free time while assuring the mother of reliable help.

Lack of dependability is probably one of the most worrisome issues related to private sitters. If a mother makes a commitment to an employer, she needs to feel certain that she can fulfill that commitment. In *The Christian Working Mother's Handbook*, author Jayne Garrison gives this advice about sitters: "To encourage regular service whether in your home or hers—pay your sitter a tad more than average and offer a bonus for 'no days missed.' "[3]

Any time a mother employs someone not previously well known to her, she has natural concerns about the quality of care. Many mothers try to keep communication lines open with their kids to ensure that the children's needs are being met and that their family's values are not in any way being compromised.

As the children get older, options include job sharing, extended hours at school in latch-key programs, and neighbors or relatives watching the kids before and after school. In some cities there are even corporate-run public schools that are open longer hours every day that local businesses are.

But many moms simply allow the kids to stay home alone. If there is more than one child in the family, some parents feel they can leave them home alone at a younger age.

There seems to be no consensus among moms about how old kids should be. Children differ in their maturity levels and in how well they can get along together without adult supervision. But some of the Christian moms we surveyed have left their kids home at least before and after school as early as the second and third grades when two siblings could be companions. Others didn't feel comfortable doing so until the kids were in the upper grades. Many said that they first left them home alone for short periods of time while Mom ran a few errands or visited a neighbor, gradually extending the time to prepare the children for more time alone.

When kids are old enough to be by themselves, some parents, instead of paying a baby-sitter, pay their children to occupy themselves peacefully while Mom is gone. If either complains about the actions of the other, neither child gets the money.

Schedule Juggling

Outside employment often requires parents to make tough choices. If Mom is going to be gainfully employed, she may have to give up something else—possibly several "something elses." Contrary to the image portrayed in the media, no one can do it all without making some compromises somewhere.

And Mom isn't the only one who will have to make sacrifices.

Schedule juggling may require sacrifice and compromise in many areas by both parents and children:

Activity level—Parents may have to tell their kids that they can't be in *all* the extra-curricular activities they would like to be involved in. Or, if they choose too many, they may have to use public transportation, and the parents may not be able to attend *all* of their performances.

One mother said that this was her key strategy as she began her summer last year—eliminate some activities so that they might relax and enjoy a few.

Sometimes our kids seem to think that time as well as money grows on trees, that there are unlimited amounts of both. Part of our responsibility as Christian parents is to teach them stewardship of both.

Work schedules—If an employer's work hours are flexible, some parents try to arrange their schedules so that one parent can be with the children until they leave for school and the other can be home as soon as possible after the kids return. Some mothers try to find evening work, especially during the summer months, so that at least one parent can be with the children most of the time. While these kinds of arrangements aren't always possible, sometimes creativity is the key to a satisfactory work/home balance.

Meal preparations—Neither husbands nor children of employed mothers should expect a hot dinner waiting on the table for them when they get home. All will need to pitch in and help.

Some mothers make multiple batches of family favorites and freeze extra portions to hasten preparation when they get home. Other parents with older grade-school kids keep the groceries on hand for easy-to-prepare meals and call home or leave instructions about how and when to start dinner.

A Minnesota nurse says that she makes up menus two weeks at a time and bases her grocery shopping on those menus. In her dining room she has a little bird with a spring-closure beak that holds a number of easy recipes and menus on cards. If she wants dinner started before she gets home, she allows the kids to pick out one of the cards and asks them to begin preparations. When they were too young for her to feel comfortable about their using the stove, her instructions might be to make a salad or some other side dish. As they grew older, they learned to make an entire meal. (For more about meal preparations, see Chapter 4 and the recipes in Appendix C.)

Sleeping patterns—Even though kids love to stay up late, as they approach adolescence they tend to need more sleep and they also love to sleep in late. Some parents, who feel it is important to ensure their kids' minimum sleep requirement, also feel it is important to maintain discipline and a fair amount of consistency between vacation and school schedules. Their personalities demand structure and predictability, and this shows up in their expectations.

Other parents are more relaxed and let their kids sleep in rather than make them get up by a certain time in the morning. They feel it doesn't matter whether the kids cram all their day's activities between 8:00 A.M. and 10:00 P.M. or between 10:00 A.M. and midnight (or whatever the specific times might be). As long as the kids still get the same amount of sleep and still interact with and contribute to the family, these parents often feel more comfortable letting the kids sleep in. Also, being awake and alone for a lesser amount of time when Mom is gone *can* mean fewer potential problems and more potential time with parents in the evening.

Sharing the Work Load

Considering the increased demands, mothers who work outside the home especially need to teach their kids survival skills. Their children often develop more independence because they frequently have to take responsibility for themselves. They learn to help with household chores because it is part of the way their family operates.

As children take more responsibility, they may also earn corresponding privileges. Many parents require that minimal chores be done before the kids are allowed certain liberties. One family requires their children's rooms be cleaned before they play or go anywhere on the weekend.

Dad's help is always welcome, too. Gone are the days of the stereotype dad in his easy chair behind the newspaper.

In spite of the fact that, on the whole, women who work outside the home still do the majority of the cooking and housework, the women we surveyed acknowledged their dependence on their husbands for support and help with the workload.

A South Dakota mother of three says, "As a working mom, I require teamwork and lots of help from my husband. He is very involved. His work hours are shorter than mine, so he fills in the gaps. He plays with the kids a lot. I couldn't do it without him."

A Missouri mother of two, who has, at times, worked more than forty hours a week during the summer, expresses similar sentiments: "My husband is a great team player. He doesn't think it is my responsibility to get the kids ready for school in the fall. We take turns taking the kids shopping for school supplies, etc."

But we can't expect our husbands to read our minds. When we need their help, we need to ask. We may get their attention by slamming cupboard doors and clanging pots and pans when we're miffed that they aren't helping, but they won't know what specifically is wrong unless we tell them.

Some suggestions for dads on how they can make life a little easier for moms during the summer may be found in the Postscript after Chapter 12 at the end of the book. You may want to add some suggestions of your own that are particularly appropriate in your family situation, but take the time to discuss your needs when you are both relaxed and in a good mood. It is less effective to photocopy the list and leave it on his dresser, or to berate him in the heat of an argument because he "never helps." You might even ask him for ideas of his own that would lighten your load.

Many families sit down together and plan who will be responsible for what, often letting kids decide which chores they would be most comfortable with. If they have a part in the decision-making, they may be slightly more willing to help.

What Do the Kids Do All Day?

One mother was frustrated when she came home from her morning class to find the milk and the breakfast dishes still on the table. "I tell my son that I expect him to be responsible and listen to my instructions," she says, "but I also feel guilty about not being there."

Often parents maintain a precarious balance on the thin line between freedom and permissiveness, between responsibility and guilt.

Jayne Garrison quotes Dr. Lee Salk, Professor of psychology and pediatrics at New York Hospital-Cornell Medical Center: "Permissiveness means no rules and regulations. But that's not caring. Children do not enjoy it, nor do they want a parent who sets no rules or standard of behavior."

Garrison goes on to say, "Children of all ages do need behavior guidelines for when we're not there to remind them. But what kind of rules and how do we enforce them when we're away from the scene?" Garrison proposes one primary rule—respect. "Respect for parents, respect for peers, respect for institutions, and respect for other's property."[4]

Following that basic rule of respect, mothers have various ways of influencing what goes on at home while they are gone. Most spell out specific rules appropriate to their family's situation and their kids' interests and activities. The list below is a compilation of several mentioned by the women we surveyed:

- No skateboarding while I am gone.
- Please write down phone messages. Be sure to get the phone number if I am to return their call.
- Bedtime is 9:30. You may camp out on the family room floor together if you wish, but no scary TV shows.
- Do not answer the door, and if anyone phones, tell them I can't come to the phone right now.
- No friends are allowed in the house while I am gone— even to go to the bathroom or get a drink (to avoid the temptation of coming in for that purpose but "accidentally" staying a little longer and starting to play. Some moms do allow playmates in the house but only when approved in advance).
- You may ride your bikes but only within the area we have agreed upon.
- If you want to go to a friend's house, you must have my permission beforehand so that I know where you are.
- You may not go into a friend's house if the parents aren't home.

Television Guidelines

Another area closely regulated in many homes when Mom is away is the TV. As long as there is a television in the home, it can be an alluring companion when parents aren't home. Yet frightening or confusing programing is often exaggerated when the kids are alone, and that's why many parents spell out explicit guidelines regarding what and how much their kids may watch. Even knowing the dangers of television, most parents choose not to get rid of it altogether. Some do, however, choose not to subscribe to special cable programing that makes R-rated movies and other highly objectionable material accessible at the flick of a switch. Children are naturally curious. It is irresponsible to put temptation in their way and then chastise them for succumbing to it.

There are *some* benefits to television. Most parents simply try to keep the boundaries clear, and take appropriate action if the kids don't follow parental guidelines. (For more about TV regulation, see Chapter 9.)

Specific Assignments

One mother of two children posts on the refrigerator a list of things the kids must do each day when they get home from school (or while she is at work during the summer). They are generally light chores, such as emptying wastebaskets, feeding and walking the dog, and scooping up droppings from the yard. But she also includes activities, such as drawing a picture for her or practicing their musical instrument. Each child must initial the items on the list as they are done. And all must be completed by the time she gets home or they forfeit certain privileges.

An Illinois mom with four children, ages nine to fifteen, leaves very specific written instructions for each child: who answers the telephone, what TV shows are allowed, what is available for snacks, and their specific bedtimes. If she has worked the previous night and needs to sleep during the morning, she leaves individual sheets of jobs for each child to complete before lunch. She says, "No child is in charge. Each child is responsible for himself or herself."

Mutual Consideration

One of the best gifts we can give our children is to be considerate. Giving them a number where we can be reached, making a point to call if we can't be home by a predetermined time, leaving instructions if we haven't talked about what to do or what there is to eat demonstrates standards of normal, considerate behavior. If we are faithful in modelling simple courtesies, we can expect them to follow our example.

Thoughtfulness is one of those traits better caught than taught. It is worth the extra effort to find our kids and tell them good-bye when we are leaving the house or to say hello to each one when we return and find out how things are going. Many moms also try to greet their children at the door when they arrive home from school, conveying the special warm welcome that says they're glad the kids are home.

Someday those patterns of courtesy and thoughtfulness will sink in to our children and it will become a part of their lives.

Communication

Moms who leave their kids home alone find good communication essential. Besides leaving the number where they can be reached and teaching their kids the importance of dialing 911 in case of an emergency, some moms also leave the phone number of a neighbor who will be home.

Communication can take on many forms. As we mentioned in Chapter 2, sometimes notes communicate better than verbal instructions or spoken words of love. Some moms like to occasionally hide little love notes in their kids' (and spouses') belongings or in their rooms to reassure them of her love. "By the time you read this, I will be working hard at the office," one might say, "but you're never far from my thoughts." Another might simply say, "I love you" or "I'm glad you're in our family."

Of course many moms also write out reminders of chores and other assignments that must be completed before she gets home. Some families have developed a message board for notes back and forth between various family members when their paths do not cross frequently enough.

Another communication tool some families use is the family activity calendar. A number of years ago the Ellises began buying large wall calendars with spaces big enough to contain several notations. The calendar hangs in a prominent place in the most popular room in the house—the kitchen. Each member of the family has a different-colored fine-tip marker, and all are responsible for writing their own activities on the calendar: band concerts or other performances, doctor's appointments, track meets, hair appointments, everything. And now that the kids are getting older, they also include their work schedules.

The calendar not only helps the family coordinate their schedules, but with each person's activities in a different color, a quick glance reveals when someone needs to slow down a bit.

The phone is also a communication lifeline. Most moms, unless their work situation prohibits it, try to remain available by phone at any time. Many make it clear that they will not settle small disputes by phone, but one mother's co-workers remarked that the tight rein she kept on her kids was the telephone cord.

Some moms even use a tape recorder to assure their kids that they're thinking about them. One mother reads to her children each night, but when she has to be gone in the evening, she prerecords the next chapter for them to listen to in her absence.

Handling Guilt and Fear

No matter how convinced parents are that becoming a two-paycheck family is a necessity, they can count on being plagued with guilt and fear. One mom said, "I notice that when acquaintances ask if I leave my children alone when I work, I always answer, 'My oldest is almost eleven!' "

Even if we don't work outside the home but have to leave our kids home alone for a few hours at a time, those feelings that we're somehow letting our kids down can really hurt. Guilt and fear immobilize. They keep us from being productive.

Each family is different, and each will make its own decisions about the work situation and how much the kids should be left alone. Choices vary according to our own priorities, circumstances, and divine leading after much prayerful consideration.

But once we walk through the door that we believe God has opened, we can't worry about other people's attitudes and remarks. We are responsible to God, and He may well remind us that some people could find something wrong with the way we are parenting our children even if we stayed home all day and never let them out of our sight.

Often the guilt we feel is false guilt—a tool of Satan to minimize our productivity. Some moms acknowledge that guilt sometimes keeps them from taking steps to correct unsatisfactory conditions at home. One mom said that she avoids mentioning rule violations when she gets home. "I probably should point them out," she says, "but I feel guilty about leaving [the kids] and don't want to get on their case right away."

Again, decisions must be carefully and prayerfully made, because guilt feelings can also serve a purpose. They may be a legitimate means of getting us to reevaluate our priorities and the amount of time we're away from our kids. One mom changed her work schedule, negotiating later work hours because she felt it was important for her to be with her kids when they got up in the morning.

Not all mothers have that kind of flexibility in their work, but whatever our choices, whatever our schedules, we can resolve to make the most of the time we do have with our kids. Being away from our kids is not necessarily synonymous with neglect.

According to research, Dr. Pat Finn, an educational psychologist, says that time is used differently in families of employed mothers. "While time spent in the presence of the mother is greater for children of nonworking mothers, time spent actually doing things together is no different. Many working mothers spend more time carpooling and driving to music lessons, ballet classes, etc., in order to minimize the effects of their absence."[5]

The question each mother must ask herself, however, is whether she realistically has sufficient energy to keep up with a job and all of that chauffeuring. Something may have to go.

Not everyone agrees with Finn's assessment. At the very least, it calls for some balance. In her article, "Good Mothers Don't Get Mad and Other Myths of Parenting," Dorothy Glasser Weiss categorizes this as the myth that quality time is more important than quantity time. "Parents cling to this myth as a way to assuage their guilt, helping them to rationalize the time they spend away from their children, or as a way to highlight the good times they share with their kids. But experts have recently become much more outspoken about the fallacy of this idea."[6]

Weiss quotes New York psychologist Dr. Simone Zelner:

There *is* "quality" in the long, humdrum days parents and children spend together.... There's something unnatural about a parent knocking herself out to spend "quality time," playing with and performing for her child almost all the time. It's like being in a courting relationship for the rest of your marriage. . . . Guilt drives many working mothers to focus too intently on their children when they're home. . . . It's more helpful to relax, and naturally go about routines at home.[7]

Priorities

Reevaluating our priorities and our family situation from time to time can keep us on the right track. One mother says she feels guilty when work comes first, but she says, "I pray that God will help me to keep my family a priority. It's easy for me to get trapped into placing work ahead of family." Occasionally, we can also try to see the situation from our kids' point of view. While my mouth says I put my family first, do I keep putting my kids off or demonstrate by my actions that I'm too busy for them? If our kids were to list our priorities, what would they put at the top?

Sometimes our kids can be one of the best barometers. Often they'll come right out and tell us that they wish we were home more. Other times, we have to be alert for more subtle symptoms.

With our feet firmly planted on scriptural principles and relying on God's strength, if we continue to demonstrate our care for our kids and clearly spell out the "while I'm gone, remember . . ." notes, what they *do* remember will be that we love them!

Looking Up

Ever-present Lord,
    be our wisdom
    in the hard decisions;
    and when we can't be
    with our kids,
    remind us that
    You are always there.
    Help us to trust them
    to Your omnipresent care.

                    Amen.

◇ 6 ◇

Preventing Atrophy of the Brain

When a muscle isn't used, it begins to deteriorate—to lose strength, to atrophy. Many parents fear that their children's *brains* will atrophy from lack of use during school breaks. While some moms and dads want their kids to have a break from academics when they're not in school, some want learning to continue.

One mom said, "I think summer and other holidays are necessary breaks for children, especially for those who are struggling. They need a chance to rebuild their self-esteem."

Another said, "Can you force children to be avid readers? I'd love to see them reading the encyclopedias in their spare time—or would I? Then I'd wonder if they were normal."

When Joyce's kids were home for 7½ weeks during a teacher's strike, she was determined to keep their minds "fit," no matter what it took. She bought math and English workbooks for all three kids at their respective grade levels and required the children to work in them each day.

While the kids got sympathy from their friends, who didn't have such "weird" mothers, the workbooks probably taught them little more than resentment. Her son says, "There's really no way of knowing if they helped us in our schoolwork when we went back, but quite honestly we hated it."

Sometimes our overzealousness can put unnecessary pressures on our kids and inhibit their creativity rather than encourage it.

Creativity

Earlier, we touched on the benefits of teaching our children survival skills, but eminent anthropologist and author Dr. Ashley Montagu adds another perspective: "Parenting that is loving teaches children not just to survive in the world, but to develop in a creatively enlarging manner, fully using their potential."[1]

He goes on to talk about activities that encourage our kids' individuality and creativity. "The need to wonder, to know and explore, to experiment, think and be creative, to sing, dance and play is as important as the need for food and shelter."[2]

Perhaps Joyce would have done just as well to take her kids on nature walks, let them explore around the lake nearby, or encourage them to play games together.

Minnesota university instructor Sharon Sheppard says that Christians are best suited to express creativity:

> As people who know the Creator personally, Christians ought to be more creative and resourceful than anyone else. We ought to be able to look at all of life through transformed minds and eyes that enable us to revel in God's universe and our position in it.[3]

Different Styles

The personalities of parents will likely affect the approaches they take to their kids' summer learning. Moms who function better in structured situations may prefer specific requirements of their kids. More laid-back mothers may take learning situations as they arise. The conflict often comes if the moms require structure of kids who are more easy going. Parents themselves can learn sensitivity to these dynamics.

A few of the moms we surveyed used workbook-style approaches during the summer. One mom said, "I have my son's study projects set up by folders: English, Math, Reading, New Words, and Adventures in the Bible. He does one or two pages per subject at a time, and I grade them."

Another mom said, "We play school, using the unused pages from the previous year's school workbooks."

Some kids *like* to play school at times and initiate it themselves, especially if they can find someone younger to be the student and they themselves can be the teachers. Workbook pages, a blackboard and chalk, an abacus, a calculator (preferably solar-powered to save on batteries), or simply paper and pencil make great props for their pretend classroom.

Another mother said, "My six-year-old daughter's teacher gave her a calendar with an activity for each summer day to keep her tuned up for fall. I really appreciated this."

The teacher suggested activities such as:

• Practice addition 1 through 10 today.
• Write a letter to a school friend.
• Go out with your dad tonight and look at the stars.
• Give another person a hug today.
• Read a book for fifteen minutes.
• Take a walk in the park and note the kinds of flowers and the kinds of bark on the trees.

Some parents sneak in a few drills, such as multiplication tables, spelling, or Scripture memory, while driving their kids around in the family taxi. But by far, the most common activities moms used for stimulating their kids' brainpower were reading related.

Expanding Our Kids' World

Award-winning author Madeleine L'Engle says,

Reading is a wonderful experience. You can go climb a tree and read all by yourself, and you're not solitary because the characters bring you into a completely new world. You become part of it, and if anyone interrupts a reader deep in his book, it's a real jolt. I almost fell out of a tree a couple of times![4]

Many moms in our survey encourage or require their kids to read at some time. Some mothers specify a time. One says, "The kids are required to read one-half hour per day." Another says, "My kids do not, by nature, curl up with a good book, so we set aside a time for all of us to read by ourselves after lunch."

At school the Ellis children became acquainted with something their teachers called S.Q.U.I.R.T.—Super Quiet Un-Interrupted Reading Time. Joyce found the concept useful at home, too. When she needed to work or the kids needed to settle down for a while, she called for SQUIRT time. It has been effective, and the fun name legitimized it in the kids' eyes.

Many parents encourage their kids to read in bed at night or in the morning if they wake up before the others. Depending on the child, Mom and Dad may have to make specific rules about *how long* the kids may stay up reading.

Some moms have general reading goals for their kids, depending on their personalities: "Our daughter reads because she likes to, but our oldest son needs to be encouraged to complete even two books per summer."

Outside help motivates some families. One mom wrote, "The library summer-reading program gets the kids started. And then they really want to read on their own." Another said, "We hired an older neighbor girl to read with our oldest son for twenty-five minutes, then ask questions for comprehension. She writes down anything she feels we need to know."

Whether reading alone or as a family, reading can entertain us, introduce us to people we never could have met, transport us to places we never could have gone, and teach us subtle truths.

Gary Rand, publisher of *Motif* magazine says,

> I don't think there's a child who has read [C. S. Lewis's] *The Lion, the Witch, and the Wardrobe* who doesn't have Christian symbolism in his being.
>
> Thousands of non-Christian kids are reading it, too. Someday when somebody comes to them and says, "God loves you and has a wonderful plan for your life," deep down in their souls they're going to remember that story, and they'll have a symbol to refer to.[5]

Much to the consternation of parents, however, many kids are not natural bookworms.

Carol, who made her childhood transitions from the school year to summer by devouring a novel a day, and sneaked a flashlight under her covers at night to finish some of them, did not give birth to children of like passions. This can be a source of frustration for any mother in that situation. Sometimes finding books on a subject our children are excited about can hook them on reading, at least to a certain extent. Reading together as a family can also spark interest in books for some kids. But it's good to remember that few people become bookworms by being forced to read.

Reading Together

One youngster whose family read together often asked, "If families don't read together, how do they know who each other's friends are?"

Truly, many families who read aloud together develop a common fun vocabulary. Those who have read Winnie the Pooh stories together may tease someone who's acting gloomy by saying he's being "Eeyorish." A hyper child might be nicknamed "Tigger." And a kid who's feeling hungry midmorning may say he feels "a little eleven-o'clockish."

Some of the Ellises' favorite books for camping trips have been the comical Pippi Longstocking books by Astrid Lindgren. Both parents and kids have great memories of hurrying into the tent at night when the mosquitoes came out; and when the family had all curled up in their sleeping bags, Mom or Dad would read by kerosene lantern light about the outlandish little girl who slept at the wrong end of the bed and could pick up her horse and set him on the front porch. Casual conversation at any time is likely to employ some of Pippi's convoluted vocabulary, such as *pluttifikation* for multiplication and *meducine* for medicine.

Frequent Trips to the Library

Fortunate is the family that lives within walking or biking distance of the public library. And doubly blessed is the family that attends a church with enough vision to provide a generous library budget and a helpful librarian.

Public libraries can be one of the finest havens for kids when they don't have school. Besides all the activities offered by many public libraries—story hours, craft lessons, films, musicians, and storytellers (ask them for their brochures)—many parents greatly appreciate the book, record, and tape resources.

To avoid problems with too many books and due dates to keep track of, some parents limit their children, for instance, to checking out only as many books as they are years old. This may require more frequent library trips if the kids are avid readers, but it can eliminate a lot of hassles. Other parents provide a special grocery-store tote box or book bag, in which library books are to be kept when not actually being read.

Libraries are also fun places to find out information. Some moms may enjoy organizing a library scavenger hunt for their kids (and maybe a few neighbor kids), offering inexpensive prizes for every one who gets all the answers right. They might give their kids historical or geographical facts to look up, such as:

- What is the capital of Uruguay?
- When did Colorado become a state?
- What is the population of New York City?
- If George Washington were still living, how old would he be today?
- Who was older when he was assassinated, President William McKinley or President Abraham Lincoln?
- Which is farther north, Minneapolis or Toronto?
- Which is taller, the Empire State Building or the St. Louis Gateway Arch?

This type of exercise can be even more fun if parents tie the questions in with the kids' current interests or topics they have studied recently in school. It can also keep children busy awhile if Mom and Dad have some of their own research or reading they need to do at the library.

Some parents let their kids investigate their proposed summer vacation spot, finding out as much as they can from the library about places to stay, points of interest, and significant historical data. Then they have the kids write letters to the department of tourism for that area to get brochures and other information, especially about particular things the kids want to see and do. One word of caution: Be sure to allow plenty of time to receive this information. (For more about traveling, see Chapter 7.)

Other Book Sources

For many kids there's something magical about owning their own books—even if the books are secondhand. One mom built a sizeable inexpensive set of Nancy Drew books for her kids through garage sales and used-book stores. Her local library periodically sold books that had been on the shelf awhile, and she found several more there. To avoid duplication, she carried in her wallet an updated list of the books they already had.

The Summer of . . .

Some kids may enjoy focusing on a particular author, series, or subject during their breaks from school. The Summer of Madeleine L'Engle, the Christmas of the Civil War, or the Narnia Spring Break are some ideas. (See Appendix D for a recommended reading list.)

Other children may go through stages, reading only mysteries for a while and then enjoying well-written historical biographies. There are a number of good Christian biographies currently available, also, which parents might suggest if the kids are in a biography phase. Christian bookstore clerks and church librarians can be helpful in finding these.

Side Benefits

Reading can also lead to learning in other areas. One grade-schooler took a special liking to a particular Christian author's series of books and decided she would copy them word for word into a notebook. Her siblings thought this was strange behavior, but her mother encouraged her. Copying quality writing verbatim is excellent training in grammar, punctuation, sentence structure, dialogue, and the flow of language.

But even if the kids don't write out the books and stories they read, any teacher can tell you that children who read or are read to frequently, do better in their other schoolwork.

Other Learning Experiences

Again, if we tried to do everything listed here, we'd go nuts and soon be struggling with guilt about what we're *not* doing. But if you see something that might work for your family on occasion, try it! Have fun.

Without wearing ourselves out, there are a number of ways to broaden our kids' understanding of different areas of life and society, such as concerts in the park, exposure to other cultures, star-gazing, or hobbies.

By watching advertisements in your local paper, you can find out about free concerts and plan ahead. Take a picnic lunch or supper and make it a special occasion.

If you're within driving distance of an Amish settlement, Chinatown, Indian reservation, or other ethnic community, you may want to spend some time there, letting your kids observe life among other cultures. If such areas are farther away, you may wish to include them in your vacation plans.

There are also a number of opportunities for families to travel to various areas of the U.S. or to other countries for short-term mission outreach or observance. You may want to check with your church or denomination to find cross-cultural experiences that may fit your family's budget and interests.

Many families enjoy lying out in the backyard together at night, finding the various constellations. You don't have to be a trained teacher to help your kids learn.

Hobbies and Skills

Carol felt frustrated with her children's lesser interest in reading until she realized that they were learning in other ways: go-cart and model-airplane building taught them practical skills and some scientific principles, such as aerodynamics—things she hadn't dreamed of teaching them.

A fifth-grade Omaha girl decided one summer that she

wanted to learn how to sew. With her mother's help, she learned how to select patterns and fabrics, lay out and cut material, and sew her own clothes. By the time she started school in the fall, she had completed two new outfits.

Some kids may become interested in doing their own sewing if parents take them shopping, noting prices in the department stores and then allowing them to browse through pattern books and bolts of material in a fabric store.

When children find out they can get two or more outfits for school or summer camp for the price of one ready-made shirt or a pair of pants, they may develop an interest. If the parents don't have sewing skills themselves, they may want to learn with their kids or let them take sewing classes.

Swimming lessons are another popular learning pursuit, especially during the summer. Some communities provide lessons to their residents at local pools or lakes for a modest cost. Many moms consider swimming not only a fun recreational activity but a survival skill—one that every child should learn.

Games—Bible and Otherwise

Sometimes, as parents, we underestimate the value of games. But authors Dean and Grace Merrill say,

> Breathes there a kid who doesn't enjoy playing a game with his parents? And breathes there a parent past fifty who doesn't regret taking so little time for games when the kids were young?
>
> Games are the parables of life. They teach us in visible ways about competing, concentrating, bearing down, not giving up, winning, losing—all vital lessons for the real world. Therefore, a family playing games together is hardly wasting time; they are enjoying one another and learning how to respond to life's realities.[6]

Bible games—trivia and other types available through Christian bookstores—can stretch our kids' biblical knowledge and keep Bible stories and principles fresh in their minds.

Other Structured Learning Experiences

Going places—Art, history, and science museums, zoos, living-history sites, and other educational places can also make learning fun. We'll discuss these more in Chapter 11.

Computers—Home computers can also take the "work" out of learning experiences. Some moms say that their kids won't touch anything that looks like homework, but their children welcome educational computer games and other software. Computers are often a worthwhile investment in view of the importance our society now places on computer skills.

"How-to" books—When one mother discovered that her daughter was interested in art, she checked out some "learn-to-draw" and "learn-to-paint" books from the library at different times. The two of them worked together, following the step-by-step lessons, and as a result both increased their sketching and watercolor skills that summer.

How-to books can also help some kids learn to crochet, knit, do counted-cross-stitch or other needlework. Sometimes parents may not have those abilities, but the kids can pick up the skills just by reading the instructions. Even if parents do know a skill, they may have their own methods that aren't easy for the kids to follow.

For example, one girl's mother crochets beautifully. She can copy nearly anything if she looks at the finished product. But written crochet directions confuse her. The daughter couldn't learn by her mother's method, but when she found some crochet instructions, she figured out how to do it on her own and now can crochet nearly anything for which she can find directions.

Nature—Many families, either in a structured way or informally, teach their kids about nature by personal observation. Mom or Dad takes the kids out to a wooded area or other natural habitat to collect such things as bugs, leaves, rocks, and wild flowers. (Beware of restrictions in government parks or privately owned areas.)

One mom said her husband took the kids out collecting, and upon their return would help them to identify their specimens and make some type of display. He would also help them discover if Scripture made mention of the things they found (e.g. ants, bees, spiders, grasshoppers, beetles, moths, sycamore, elm, juniper, chestnut, rose, thistle. You can check a concordance for references.).

Television? A Learning Tool?

Does TV prevent atrophy of the brain or contribute to it? Most of us are so used to hearing television bad-mouthed that the idea of television as a positive force sounds like heresy. But noted author and family specialist Dr. Howard Hendricks of Dallas Theological Seminary recognizes that TV can be a learning tool. In his article, "Can TV Be Effective for Education?" he basically says it can *if*:

- it is controlled, restricted, and regulated
- parents know what their children are watching
- programs are evaluated afterward.

He lists some of the advantages of TV:

> It helps us visualize concepts, events, and experiences. It makes past events come alive, and it allows us to travel to places we will never visit in person. Television, particularly educational programs and documentaries, answers basic questions. It presents models—some negative and some positive. It expands our world experience.[7]

Some of the parents we surveyed particularly saw value in educational game shows, cultural events, documentaries, the relatively rare "clean" family sitcom, and nature specials.

Jerry Jenkins, writer-in-residence at Moody Bible Institute, brings a word of balance when he says, "It's amazing how much discussion is necessary even after educational shows, which generally ignore the creator and espouse evolution."[8]

Besides the objections we have to some of the programing on TV, parents are often concerned about the constant barrage of commercials convincing us that we can't live without certain products we never knew we needed before.

Television reviewer Noel Holston makes an interesting point about TV's encouragement of greed. He says,

> The most insidious way commercial TV attempts to persuade us that we always need something new, something improved or just something else is by making it appear that virtually everybody else already has those things. The message is not just in the commercials, it's imbedded in the many conspicuously affluent programs. I'm not talking about "Lifestyles

of the Rich and Famous." On the tube of plenty, the lifestyles of the anonymous are none too shabby, either.[9]

Other objectionable elements include the promos for programs we wouldn't want our children to see or for R-rated movies "coming soon to a theater near you." Usually the promos show the most titillating clip from the program or movie.

This is our opportunity as parents to ask questions and discuss (not preach about) the values being portrayed. Sometimes a little sarcasm or humor handles commercials best: "Now see, all you have to do is use that kind of toothpaste, and you'll fall in love" or "Right, who would drink a diet soft drink—*just for the taste of it*?"

In his previously cited article, Jerry Jenkins, known for his wonderful wit, says,

> The only way I know how to fight the bad influence of TV commercials is to help the kids change the lyrics to the songs. Instead of "a beer you can believe in," they sing, "A beer you can go blind with." And so on. That's one way to counteract harmful values.[10]

When we're offended by something on TV, we as parents also have the right to switch channels or turn the TV off for thirty seconds or a minute until the program we *wanted* to watch begins again.

If a family likes to post scripture verses around the house, Psalm 101:3 would be a good one atop the television set: "I will set before my eyes no vile thing."

We can also point out good commercials, commenting on their clever stunts or writing. We don't want to always be negative.

Fine-tuning TV Use

Knowing the pros and cons of television, most of the mothers we surveyed had found a comfort level in their family's TV use. Some had strongly negative views of television and allowed their kids little viewing time, while others showed a bit more tolerance. The amount these families watched TV ranged from virtually none to three or four hours a day. The majority of homes surveyed averaged between thirty minutes and two hours.

That falls right in line with the American Academy of Pediatrics' recommendation of "a maximum of one to two hours a day for all children."[11]

But each family needs to decide what is a workable amount for them and stick to it. In a 1990 speech about TV-viewing habits, Kevin Carrier, a Luther College student from Guttenberg, Iowa, said that you can tell you've been watching too much television when you start relating real-life events to something you saw on TV—as though *that* were reality.

One of the world's most respected authorities on the family, Cornell University's Dr. Urie Bronfenbrenner, says,

> The primary danger of the TV screen lies not so much in the behavior it produces as in the behavior it prevents—the talk, the games, the family activities, and the arguments through which much of the child's learning takes place and his or her character is formed.[12]

Suggestions for Positive TV-viewing

Below are a number of ideas parents have used to control their television use. You may want to try one or two with your family.

Two things at once—Encourage children to engage in other activities while watching TV: folding laundry, ironing, putting a puzzle together, handcrafts/needlework/sewing, cleaning, peeling potatoes, hobbies, exercising (jogging trampoline or other kind of exercise).

Marking the television listing—Browse through the weekly listing at the beginning of the week and agree upon which shows may be watched. Use a highlighter to mark them, and allow children to watch only those programs. This is especially important for mothers who work outside the home.

Tickets—Buy or let your kids make tickets, each representing one-half hour of television viewing. Decide how much television you want your children to watch over the period of a week. (It could vary from week to week, depending on programing.) Issue the appropriate number of tickets to each child at the beginning of the week. Whenever children watch television, require them to deposit their tickets in a can or box with a slit in the top. When the kids' tickets are gone, they cannot watch any more television. (Tickets can be reused from week to week.)

Consequences—When television privileges are abused, children forfeit an equal (or double) amount of viewing the next day (or week).

Family event—Some television programing may call for a special occasion. You might want to have a picnic in your TV room while watching the televised Olympics or another noteworthy event.

Watch together—As often as possible, watch TV with your kids or at least remain close-by so that you can monitor what they're hearing and seeing. Exercise your prerogative to turn off the TV when necessary.

Consistency with flexibility—Generally stick to your plan for the amount and types of programing you feel is right for your family, but be flexible if kids have used up their time and an unannounced special comes on at the end of the week that the kids want to see or you would like them to see. (Make sure they know this is an exception to the rule.)

TV can be a positive educational tool if it is regulated, monitored, and evaluated. Many parents have found their comfort zone and are keeping television in its place.

Learning—Outside of School?

While parents are divided about formal learning activities, we would probably all agree that we learn things every day through various means depending upon our personalities.

As long as our kids are having fun exercising their curiosity, exploring new ideas, and discovering the world around them—in *whatever* ways we're comfortable with—we can be sure that their brains won't atrophy. They'll actually grow!

Looking Up

Lord,

> _Keep us alert_
> _to learning opportunities_
> _for our kids,_
> _but remind us_
> _that You,_
> _Omniscient God—_
> _not we,_
> _are the Source_
> _of all knowledge._

Amen.

◇ 7 ◇

Close Encounters of the
Traveling Kind

C ar travel may be one of the most challenging activities
families dare. (Is that putting it mildly?) Defying all common sense, suffering memory lapses about "last time," or simply being unable to afford any other way to get from point A to point B, we take our lives and sanity in our hands as we grip the steering wheel and head across country to visit grandparents or to have a "fun" vacation.

The stress level is often so high that some families avoid long trips altogether, preferring more frequent, shorter ones.

Why is traveling so often a disaster?

Submarine Syndrome

A number of years ago, Carol planned a trip to the West Coast with her parents and adult siblings to attend a wedding. Someone suggested renting a large van and traveling together. Their father, a World War II Navy veteran, vetoed the idea. "Separate cars in caravan," he said.

They honored his request.

En route, Carol asked him about the veto.

"It would have been *too much* togetherness," he replied. "I learned that aboard Navy submarines. No matter how nice people are, you need some space."

Aboard a submarine in WW II he didn't have the option of separate vehicles. Traveling with his adult children, he did. So he exercised a little preventive spacing.

When children are younger and don't have their own vehicles (or even a driver's license), submarine syndrome is a definite risk. A family, no matter how close, is not used to the amount of togetherness a car trip demands.

Traveling with children requires preventive spacing. It takes such forms as frequent breaks and items brought along to occupy the kids—games, books, tapes, activity books, markers. (See Appendix E for extensive list of resources and other suggested items to keep your kids busy on long trips—any trip can be long if the kids aren't happy.)

But *immunotherapy* can also help parents avoid many of the potential problems of the submarine syndrome. What does immunotherapy entail?

First, be reasonable in goals and expectations. From the moment we begin planning a vacation, we need to remind ourselves that this is a *family* vacation, not a *parental* one. (A parental vacation is when we can occasionally steal a weekend alone with our spouse, leaving our children in someone else's care. There are never enough of those, are there?) As long as we are with our children, we have the privilege and responsibility of being their models, guides, and disciplinarians, and we act accordingly.

Second, accept reality. Despite the glowing report we will probably bring back about our vacation, not every moment will go smoothly and perfectly. We will probably take some wrong turns, get caught in traffic jams, sweat in the hot sun, and experience some sibling squabbles.

Finally, determine a sense of purpose about the vacation. Ask yourself what you're hoping to accomplish on this trip. Relax with simple goals like: taking a break from our usual high-pressure routine, enlarging our children's experience by seeing other parts of the country, fostering a sense of family unity and identity.

With those goals in mind, we won't try to take in the maximum number of sites in a minimum number of hours. That wouldn't accomplish our goals. It would only make everyone tired, which would probably lead to crankiness and squabbles. When we forget our goals, is it any wonder we often return home from vacation feeling too tired to go back to work the next day?

With realistic goals in mind, we can try to learn together all we can about the places we do visit, perhaps reading a guidebook together in the car or taking time to read historical markers along the way as well as discussing what we've seen.

After a long day of fighting New York City traffic and seeing many homeless people, Carol's six-year-old said, "Know what I learned? I learned how good we have it at home."

Planning ahead with some simple goals enables us to take advantage of opportunities to talk with our children about things that interest them and are important to them. Hectic schedules at home seldom afford such luxury.

Some of Joyce's favorite memories of family trips are the times after dark when all the kids were asleep except one. Mom and Dad could zero in on that one child, who often initiated conversation, opening up more readily in the still darkness than at any other time.

Ideas to Help the Miles Zip By (Well, Almost)

Chart your course—Some automobile clubs provide tour books for their members, plotting the best course to reach your destination. Take advantage of these. They also list interesting things to see and do (often at little or no cost). Some even include discount coupons.

Try letting the kids take turns in the front passenger seat as navigator, watching the map for upcoming towns and cities or the next highway to take. This helps them envision the geography of the area in a way they'll never forget. One mother said, "Our youngest is a real geography and map buff. Following his atlas, he kept us informed of upcoming sights, elevations, and the population of every little town along the way."

Individual amusements—Help or encourage each child to pack an activity bag with small toys, games, activity books, pads of paper, pencils, markers, reading books, and a favorite small stuffed animal or doll. (The previous year's school bag works well—often its last hurrah—or stitch simple bags from leftover fabric, making handles that hook over the headrests of the front seat to allow more leg room for your kids. You could also recycle plastic shopping bags for this purpose.) Require kids to return the things they have been playing with to the bag before something else is taken out, thus reducing clutter.

Some parents wrap inexpensive gifts or toys in bright wrapping paper, allowing the children to unwrap one each day. This is particularly fun on long family trips during the Christmas holidays but works well at other times, too.

Other moms and dads let an older child pack the activity bag for a younger sibling, thus providing enjoyment for both as the younger child discovers what's in there. This can foster thoughtfulness, too, as the older one has to really think about someone else's likes, dislikes, and needs.

Beware of crayons for traveling. The same warning about pets in closed cars applies to wax crayons. As your vehicle sits in the hot sun, crayons can ooze all over, making a terrible mess. Water soluble markers are a better choice.

Take along an extra notebook or tablet for each child. Each night, when you stop at a motel or campground to rest, let the children paste into their notebooks the postcards, ticket stubs, nature findings, or whatever else they collected during the day. They can also write something they want to remember about what they did. Children who can't write can dictate to Mom or Dad or draw pictures. These notebooks bring back pleasant memories years afterward.

Shared amusements—music—Cassette tapes are a common favorite with traveling families. Let the kids have input about what tapes to take so that there is music to suit each person's taste. Sing-along tapes are often popular, especially with younger children.

Some families keep a hymnal or two in the car for trips of any length. Car travel is a great time to learn the words to some of the great hymns of our Christian heritage. Let the kids follow along in the hymnal(s) while Mom and Dad sing from memory. Kids love to catch us in our mistakes (or momentary memory lapses), and the challenge is good for us as parents. Gospel songs and praise choruses also provide an opportunity to focus on our Creator, Savior, and Lord. A side benefit: Somehow it's tough to remain grumpy when everyone around you is singing!

Other tapes—There are many books available on tape now, novels and nonfiction, that can captivate the attention of children and adults for hours. Stretch your kids' minds with some of the classics like *Anne of Green Gables* or *Treasure Island*. Often when children hear a book read or dramatized, it whets their appetite to read it when they are old enough. Concordia's Arch Books Aloud and other Bible stories on tape match the younger child's attention span, and the lively rhymes, background music, and sound effects make them favorites.

Old radio programs are also fun and give our children a frame of reference when they hear someone talking about Abbott and Costello's "Who's on First?" routine or Jack Benny's miserly ways. They are part of our culture.

If your children have a dramatic flare, encourage them to spend some of the time before your vacation taping their own renditions of radio shows for listening fun during the trip.

Shared memories—If you tend to procrastinate about putting photos into albums, take them along on your trip, and let the kids arrange pictures in the albums while enjoying memories of people, places, and events of the past—near or distant.

Electronic communication—Communicating with other travelers by C.B. radio can be lots of fun for children and adults. This is especially enjoyable when friends or relatives are traveling together in caravan. Adults can keep in touch regarding places to stop as well as keeping each other alert with chatter and jokes—if they can wrestle the C.B. away from their kids. A C.B. radio can keep children busy for hours.

Games

Billboard alphabet—Each person watches the billboards, calling out (or writing down, for a quieter game) words that begin with each letter of the alphabet in order, for example: "Amoco for A," "Bargain for B." If playing aloud, the same word can't be used more than once unless it appears more than once. See who can get through the alphabet first. For a variation, try it with letters on license plates.

Your turn—One child begins a story, stops at a crucial point, and the next person has to continue the tale. Mom and Dad can join in, too.

License plate—See how many different states and provinces you can find represented by license plates. Children may want to keep track on paper. Another game requires making three-word sentences from the three letters of a license plate number: DYF 739 could be *D*ial *Y*our *F*riend. Use your imagination to come up with other license plate games.

Don't forget old favorites—"Twenty Questions" (some people call it Animal-Vegetable-Mineral), "I See Something," and "Who Am I?"—especially good with Bible characters, provide fun ways to pass the traveling hours.

Handling Boundary Disputes and Other Squabbles

In the other guy's shoes—When two of Carol's boys were fighting over territorial rights in the back seat, one drew a line, obviously giving himself more room. When Mom asked if he thought he had made a fair division of space, he said yes. But when she suggested they trade places, the line drawer reconsidered and compromised on the line location. Peace reigned (at least for a while).

Rotation—Simply switching places frequently helps in some families. Joyce's family often arranges suitcases in the rear section of the station wagon so that they can make a bed (using several thicknesses of blankets or afghans) just big enough for one person. Then the kids take turns being in the back and enjoy a little more privacy.

Energy-release breaks—One mom says the most she can hope for is one to two hours of relative quiet in the car with her children before the restlessness and fighting become unbearable. She and her husband found that frequent stops—a service station for a cold drink, Dairy Queen for ice cream, a park for lunch, or a chance to run and play at a rest area—helped with energy release. Although it stretched an eight-hour trip to ten or eleven, they felt that eleven hours of comparative peace beat eight hours of frazzled nerves.

Company halt!—Another family stops at the side of the road whenever squabbles break out, refusing to start the car again until the bickering stops.

"Heads, it's yours for five minutes"—When one mom's boys were fighting over who got to play with G.I. Joe, she took it away, promising to give it back when they could agree on how to share. After twenty minutes, they realized she was serious and decided on five-minute turns, the first possession being determined by the flip of a coin.

Money-handling Ideas

Cutting costs—Some families find meals one area in which they can economize most easily—eating out for only one meal a day. One mother says, "We eat a cold breakfast in our motel room, eat lunch from a cooler we've packed, and then dine out in the evening. Another way to save money is to pack a jug of ice water in the car rather than stopping frequently to buy soft drinks.

A mealtime game—In Birkey and Turnquist's book *Building Happy Memories and Family Traditions*, one mother tells this story: "When taking our six children on a trip, we have a game we play in restaurants. Each in turn orders his meal and hands the menu to the waitress, remembering the price of one another's orders, so they can guess what the total bill will be. The one guessing closest wins a prize of a dollar. In the meantime, all six are quiet, orderly, and beginning to realize what it takes for a family of eight to eat out."[1]

Avoiding "souvenir beggars"—Many families insist that the children take their own money on trips for souvenirs, which eliminates a lot of begging and teaches them management skills. If they spend it all at the first souvenir shop, they have nothing more for the rest of the trip.

Other Helpful Pointers

Prepare children for what's ahead—As often as possible, lay out the day's schedule for your kids, so they know what to expect. Author Carol K. Halmrast also suggests giving each child a map or atlas and laying it out on the table before leaving on the trip so that the children can visualize the geography and follow the route as you travel.

Remember, kids are used to structure at school. They'll respond better if they know what's ahead, especially if they have some input. This doesn't eliminate spontaneity. Be flexible, but don't forget that advance warning is also helpful.

Before you leave the car to swim at an inviting beach, tour a historic site, or enjoy some other activity, be sure the kids know what is expected of them. If you wait until they are in public, in the middle of the activity, or later when they're tired or excited, it's harder to reason with them.

Consider underlying causes—One mother became frustrated with the bickering about who got to put their feet where. Then she realized how long it had been since they had eaten. After stopping for a quick roadside picnic with nutritious food, peace reigned for the next 100 miles.

Remember, too, that when parents are facing forward, they can't see everything that's going on in the back. A lot of needling can occur out of your sight, and the one who complains or whines (the one who often gets disciplined) may be the victim, not the instigator. Try keeping the visor mirror down to give you eyes in the back of your head.

Remain sensitive—Sometimes when parents are trying to read or work on projects of their own in the car, it's easy to overlook the immediate needs of the kids. On one trip Carol had been reading for half an hour when her young son walked his teddy bear up her arm and onto her shoulder. Then the bear turned a book page and nuzzled her face. She looked up. "Does your bear need some attention?" she asked. "No, but I do," her son replied. She closed the book.

Mission Accomplished?

Vacation trips, while never perfect, can be successful. One mother said, "For our family, the important fact isn't so much what we do for fun and entertainment but that everyone enjoys it and that we do it together." That's refreshing in a world where differing schedules often pull us apart. Another mom made it even more practical: "I found my children can play nicely together—at a motel pool."

And not everyone will get the same thing out of the vacation. "We thought our young girls would be impressed with the Colorado Rockies and all the beautiful lakes and rivers," another parent wrote. "What gave them the greatest joy? The chipmunks they fed, the butterflies they watched, the pretty stones they collected, and the wildflowers they picked. We were impressed by the distant majesty, but they were captivated by the beauty right at their fingertips—beauty we had passed by."

Regardless of the inevitable squabbles along the way, if we have reasonable goals and expectations, accept the realities of "close encounters," and maintain our sense of purpose, each trip can be called a success.

——————— *Looking Up* ———————

Lord,

> *We need rest sometimes—*
> *a change of pace,*
> *a change of scenery,*
> *admiring Your creation,*
> *simply having fun,*
> *but remind us that*
> *togetherness*
> *is more important*
> *than itinerary.*
> *And oh, God of peace,*
> *help us find*
> *our ultimate rest*
> *in You.*

Amen.

◇ **8** ◇

Time for Mom

Personal time?" asked one of the moms in our survey. "What's that?"

Another said, "I do not find enough personal time. I think my kids hear me open my eyes in the morning. I'm glad they are eager to see me right away, but I need to be alone sometimes, too."

Most of the women surveyed acknowledged a need for time alone but few found it—at least on a regular basis. High on their priority list was time alone with God.

In Search of . . . A Quiet Time

For many mothers, trying to have daily devotions is like trying to mate every sock in the laundry basket. Many Christian women (and men) struggle to carve out that special time with the Lord each day. And when the kids are home, mothers often wonder how they can find half an hour for a quiet time when they can't find five minutes alone for any kind of quiet.

Numerous moms who took part in the survey expressed their frustration in this area. One said, "I have a hard time finding time for devotions. Daytime is full of constant interruptions from my grade-schoolers. But my teenagers keep late hours, making evenings difficult, too. Lately, I've tried to squeeze time in before bed. Yet my mind and body are exhausted at that point."

Occasionally, when we do get alone with our Bible, our minds wander. We can't concentrate. Often we feel spiritually malnourished. Most Christian moms recognize that a special time away from radios, stereos, TV, and other people's demands is absolutely essential. This is our time to communicate with the Lord. It is His time to strengthen us.

Sometimes we just need someone to talk to—someone who won't think us unspiritual for thoughts and attitudes that creep into our minds. We can talk to God because He knows about them anyway. And *He* can change us.

Some days it's easy to understand the mother who runs away from her family when pressures become too great—if she doesn't have the Lord to fortify her. Moms need the wisdom, patience, and endurance that can only come from God.

One mom wrote, "To be organized, I must have some of my own time each day, a quiet time. I'm a better mother if I do. I can't give my kids *all* my time or I go crazy. And they don't need a crazy mom!"

So, acknowledging that we need that time of communication and strengthening, how is it structured? And how can we find the time?

What's It Like?

First, it is important to realize that the terms, *quiet time, personal devotions*, or *morning watch*, as some people call it, are not in the Bible. Therefore, we can't look to Scripture for a blueprint of what a quiet time should be like. But God's Word is full of examples of people communing with God, spending time in His presence, talking to God, and listening to Him. So the common practice of a quiet time has two main ingredients: prayer (we talk to God) and meditation on Scripture (God talks to us). Beyond that, there's a great deal of flexibility.

Each of us responds to God differently because of the differences in our personalities. Each mother's quiet time is her own. No one will occupy a lesser place in heaven because she doesn't "do" hers like someone else's. We can imagine that our Lord, the Creator of the universe, is delighted when we creatively devise time with Him that is uniquely ours.

The moms we surveyed gave us some of the ingredients in their devotional times:

One mother said she was trying to read through the Bible in a year, underlining as she went. Another uses the *Word of Life Quiet Time Diary*, which has a Scripture-reading schedule for one year and a place for a prayer diary. Still another said, "I spend most of my time talking with the Lord—telling Him what is going on and how I feel about it. The Lord often helps me know the right way to look at a situation. Time in His Word is important to me, too. Often a Bible verse comes to mind at the right time to help me."

Because some moms struggle with quiet-time ideas, here are a few general guidelines and specific suggestions, which we hope will spark other workable ideas for each individual:

Find a time and place—When the kids are home, finding a workable time and place seems like the impossible dream! But we can usually be a bit more consistent if we choose a time and place that "works" for us. One mother may be more alert at night and prefer to have her time with the Lord then. A mother of three says, "I get my personal time only after the kids are in bed, and that is always 10:00."

Another mother may find that after doing five loads of laundry in between chauffeuring her children and arbitrating endless sibling wars, she is too exhausted to concentrate on the Scriptures or stay awake during prayer. She discovers that by getting up a half hour earlier for that purpose, her mind is fresher. Among the moms we surveyed, morning seemed the most popular for quiet times.

One said, "My husband leaves for work at 5:30, so I stay up and have my devotions then." Another said, "I try to get up half an hour before the kids to read, meditate, and organize my day."

Some moms may find that having burned the candle at both ends for too long, their only good time is the middle of the day. They may call for quiet reading or play after a meal, assigning each child to a different room, in order to give themselves some solitude with God.

The more structured mom will often plan her time alone as though it were an appointment to which she must not even be a moment late. One mother says, "My key to having devotions is to plan a regular time. No planning, no devotions."

Another mom writes, "I find that personal devotions have to be planned, otherwise I miss them. I like to have them at my desk in my bedroom. I close the door, and if the kids disturb me, I say, 'Please let me finish my time with God.' I think this helps them see that spending time with God is important to me."

She adds another sentence in parentheses, however, which is an encouragement to those of us who aren't quite that disciplined: "(It doesn't always happen this way. I keep working at it.)" Some moms make plans but realistically allow for differences in their schedule. "I get up early," another mom says. "But I can't do this every day, so I plan early morning devotions when I can, and enjoy them immensely. And I refuse to feel guilty when I can't or don't."

The spontaneous mom may exchange her unrealistic goal of a fixed time in a certain place for trying to remain alert for snatches of time throughout the day—while the kids are outdoors playing or other moments of relative peace among the troops.

We can get direction from the Lord even in finding our time to meet with Him alone. If we ask Him to clear one segment (or several little snatches) of time to be with Him, He'll show us where those times are.

He looks forward to that time with us, too!

A notebook can help—Because it's often hard to be disciplined in our time with God or to even remember where we were reading from one day to the next, some people use a notebook to focus their thoughts during their devotional time.

An 8½ × 11 spiral-bound notebook or stenographer's pad works well. Many people have their own ways of journaling their devotional thoughts, but here is one way you may find useful in using a notebook as a quiet time tool:

Label each page with the day and date—On the first line write the word PRAISE. Skip two lines, then write PRAYER. Skip two more lines and write PASSAGE. This outline can focus your communication with God and provide balance.

Begin—Start with a short prayer, asking the Lord to direct your thoughts and show you what He wants you to see in His Word for that day. Then begin filling in the outline.

Under PRAISE honestly express your gratitude as you concentrate on the Lord's character and His daily gifts to you. For instance: "Lord, I praise You that You never leave me, even when I get frustrated with the kids and don't handle their squabbles the way I think I should," or "Lord, thank You for the rain today, even if it means inside activities for the kids. I know the crops really need it," or "Lord, thank You for my husband's sensitivity last night in taking the kids to the park so that I could have some time alone after a terrible day at work."

Under PRAYER, write out a short prayer of petition—something specific you want to ask the Lord for that day: "Lord, please give me patience as ten of Tommy's friends come to our house for a birthday lunch today," or "Lord, today Becky leaves for her first week away at summer camp. Please calm the butterflies in her stomach (and mine)," or "Lord, please help Bobby to be more patient with Kimmy. She doesn't *mean* to ruin his toys. She's *so* little."

You don't have to be eloquent. What you write is just between you and God. He's more interested in honesty than eloquence.

Then, by the word PASSAGE jot down the Scripture you have chosen to read that day, such as James 1:1–8. It's best to start at the beginning of a book and work your way through it. Skipping around tends to develop spiritual indigestion. One of the Gospels (such as Mark or John) or one of the shorter epistles (such as Philippians or Colossians) is a good place to start. Break your reading into small portions. Since your time is often limited, especially when the kids are home, you'll want to think through what you're reading and make notes.

Answer questions for yourself, such as: What is the main teaching of this passage? What other applications could I make to my daily routine and thought patterns today? What can I learn about *sin*, here? What does it teach me about my *Savior*? What is God trying to show me about *service* for Him? These three "s's" can help you relate the passage to your own personal situation.

You may also want to copy verses you will memorize onto 3×5 cards and place them in highly visible areas—like above the kitchen sink!

Note unfamiliar words, seeming contradictions, or anything you don't understand. Later, consult a dictionary, Bible commentary, or your pastor or spiritual mentor for clarification.

You don't have to use the whole page, or you may fill several. It's *your* quiet time. Writing things down simply helps us remember them better and provides a record of what the Lord has taught us.

Those who have to catch snatches of time during the day for spiritual refreshment often enjoy a notebook system like this because it gives them something to come back to. It helps them regain their train of thought if the telephone rings or their kids spill a gallon jug of red Kool-Aid on the carpet. Some interruptions are inevitable.

As you're finishing your quiet time, you may want to write at the bottom of the page the word PERSONAL. Under this heading you can write a prayer thought, responding to what the Lord has shown you from Scripture. Sometimes a "personal" prayer can be simply one of adoration: "Lord, when I see what You did for me on the cross, all I can say is, 'I love You!' "

Sometimes it's a prayer for direction: "Lord, You've reminded me this morning that You want me to be a witness for You. I think I'll invite Jennifer over for coffee today while our kids play together in the pool. Guide me so that I may introduce You to Jennifer as well as to my own kids—my 'home' mission field."

Another such prayer might be: "Lord, thank You for showing me that You really *do* care about the smallest things in my life. Help me to truly cast all my burdens on You." Then list specific areas that are a particular burden at that moment.

Sometimes this prayer might be a difficult one of confession: "Lord, You've shown me that I've been envious of the way Margaret's kids seem to help around the house so willingly. I haven't even wanted to go over there lately. Help me set things straight and make her my friend again."

As we weave the Scriptures into our thinking and living, God's strength and wisdom will be there as we need them.

After time in God's Word, it's good to pray for other people and concerns. You may find it helpful to categorize your list: friends, relatives, neighbors, church leaders, missionaries, government leaders. If you write your list on the inside cover of your notebook, you can easily pray for one category each day.

If your scripture meditation exhausts your allotted time, keep the day's "category" in mind and pray while you're vacuuming, folding towels, or mopping up the spilled Kool-Aid.

Set realistic goals—"It's important not to be legalistic in your quiet time," said the late author, Paul Little. "At the same time it shouldn't be totally *laissez faire*. A lot of people, in their desire to be disciplined, end up in bondage. If they don't get in their twelve and a half minutes in study, and four minutes and twelve seconds in prayer, they're going to get hit with a car and stars will fall out of heaven. . . . Stars aren't going to fall out of heaven if a quiet time is missed one day, but if week after week goes by with only a snack on Sunday and a little refreshment on Wednesday, there will be trouble."[1]

One mom found that she had to set modest, more realistic goals for her quiet time, sometimes experimenting with only three times a week. Although it seemed heretical, three times a week was better than none. Before long, as she saw the Lord strengthen and change her in that time together with Him, she couldn't wait until her next quiet time.

One mom had to reduce the amount of time she allotted for devotions. "I take 10–15 minutes in the morning now," she says. "I have finally learned to scale down my expectations, so I will do them regularly. *For me* regularity is important because I notice a big difference in my day and attitudes if I start the day with God and am aware of His presence."

The system or schedule we use isn't as important as the commitment to two-way communication with God. If we spend time with Him on a regular basis, we will be changed!

The Heart of Communing With God

But for all these thoughts on the mechanics of a quiet time, we would do well to remember Andrew Murray's warning in *The Believer's Daily Renewal* about the "danger of substituting prayer and Bible study for living fellowship with God—the living interchange of giving Him your love, your heart, and your life, and receiving from Him His love, His life, and His spirit."[2] Murray warns of letting the Word of God become a substitute for God himself. "This is the greatest hindrance to fellowship because it keeps the soul occupied instead of leading it to God himself."[3]

Many of us struggle with the feeling that our quiet times, when we have them, are too me-centered. We read Scripture to find out what *we* can get from it. We go over our prayer requests as if we were handing Santa our Christmas wish list. And so, we strive to make our devotions a time of personal worship, focusing on God.

Again, Andrew Murray gives great insight. "What nobility would come into life if secret prayer were not only an asking for some new sense of comfort, or light, or strength, but also the surrendering of life just for one day into the sure and safe keeping of a mighty and faithful God."[4]

That gives a much different perspective to our days when the kids are home.

Other Personal Time

While a few moms (very few) in our survey felt comfortable with the amount of time they had to themselves, they admitted that that was part of their personalities. One mom said, "I don't need a lot of time to myself. I don't like crowds, but I don't mind family members around."

Probably more of us can empathize with the mom who said,

"I still haven't figured out a time for *me*."

We all need *some*. Here are a few suggestions the women we surveyed came up with:

Exercise—The mom who said she got up with her husband at 5:30 to have her devotions says she then "bikes to the river and back before the kids wake up."

Another says, "I walk twenty minutes each evening, and my children take turns walking with me."

Getting away—This can be a vacation alone or with our husbands. But more often, it is a few hours (minutes?) by ourselves or even a "mental vacation."

Some mothers enjoy a women's Bible study get-away for a weekend. "How good it is to forget home responsibilities for a time!" says one mom. "I came home refreshed and reminded how good a break is for me, my husband, and my children."

Another mother simply checked into a bed & breakfast for a couple of days to recoup. "I had to sacrifice elsewhere in the budget to afford it, but I needed it badly," she said. "I spent most of my time reading and enjoying God's beautiful creation. By the way," she adds, "I've only done that once."

Other quick escapes some moms use:

- Sit down and drink a glass of orange juice.
- Lie down for ten minutes.
- Take a short, brisk walk.
- Play the piano for 10–15 minutes.
- Take a bubble bath.
- Sip iced tea on a porch swing and talk to God.
- Watch TV with your arms wrapped around your kids.

Getting away is often even more difficult for mothers who work outside the home, but sometimes a lunch break can be a mini-vacation. In Jayne Garrison's book *The Christian Working Mother's Handbook*, she offers these lunchtime vacation suggestions:

Prepare for your journey by scanning city brochures and newspapers for places you've never been that are within reasonable distance of your office. Then make a list. Perhaps you'll eat lunch at that tiny Mexican cafe you've always wondered about. Maybe you'll visit a vintage clothing store and purchase something nostalgically romantic. Could be you'll walk to City Hall or rest your feet beside a "downtown" fountain. The key is to shed inhibitions and explore.[5]

.She also suggests riding the bus instead of driving, taking advantage of "waiting time" for personal reading or letter writing, closing your office door during lunch to dim the lights and put your feet up, and listening to soothing Christian or classical tapes while commuting.

Moms who don't work outside the home can do many of those things, too.

Time with friends—For some reason some mothers feel more isolated during the summer and need to push themselves to get together with friends so that they aren't so in-grown as a family. How we all need time with friends—when there's no hidden agenda!

One mom started an evening Bible study for fellow working women with a simple question-and-answer study and sharing of prayer requests. "It doesn't substitute for one-on-one sharing, but it helps to know that others are praying," she says.

Another mother visits by phone. She says, "I grab a moment when I can to make a quick telephone call to say hi. It doesn't take long, and ten minutes of sharing on the telephone does wonders to revive a friendship, especially if they know I called just to talk."

Still another said that sometimes she simply has to call a friend and say, "Please come over for lunch tomorrow. The house is a mess, but I really want to see you and spend some time together."

One mom sums it all up, saying, "Friends are the only way a young, homebound mother stays sane."

Personal enjoyment—We all need some time for letter writing, reading, and pursuing personal interests. One mother, who enjoys sewing, says, "My personal time is late at night alone with my European pattern books, planning this fall's wardrobe for us all." To some moms that might be work. To her, it's enjoyment.

Another mother writes, "I try to get a couple hours of 'my time' on Sunday to read, write letters, etc. It usually works if I first spend a couple hours with my children doing what they like. Then when I announce it is my time, they usually respect it."

A mother of four grade-schoolers says, "Two afternoons a week I hire a high-school student to take the kids to the pool so that I have some catch-up time by myself."

Some moms need to find room for hobbies. One says, "I'm always trying to find more time to paint. This morning I woke at 5:30 and painted one and a half hours, then slept half an hour. That worked OK. I may try it again."

Even a short, leisurely walk can be a time of personal enjoyment. After walking just three familiar blocks, Carol jotted down her thoughts: "I've driven that road hundreds of times and never saw the quaint retaining wall, the pine tree with thousands of cones forming, the curve in the road. Walking gave me new eyes. I want to do more walking, less driving in life."

Balance

A few final points can help us keep balance in our quest for personal time:

- Remind yourself to take time alone when you need it. There seems to be a natural tension between me-ism and healthy time to ourselves. But that tension is good. It keeps us alert to straying too far in either direction.
- Ask your husband, children, and friends for help. A number of the mothers we surveyed indicated that their husbands were quite helpful when asked. But we can't expect them to read our minds or automatically know when we need this time.
- Be alert for opportunities. Too often we miss chances for personal time because we're not looking for them. Afterward, (like the old V–8 commercial), we hit our head and say, "I could have had some time to myself!"
- Rejoice when you find personal time; relax and enjoy! Don't let false guilt, anyone, anything rob you of your joy.
- Don't complain if you don't get enough time for yourself. For some of us, there's probably never enough. Thank the Lord for the personal time you find, and trust Him to provide more when you need it.

_____ *Looking Up* _____

Lord,

> *We need and enjoy time*
> *with our family;*
> *we need and enjoy time*
> *to ourselves,*
> *but help us enjoy*
> *to the fullest*
> *whatever time we have*
> *with You.*
> *Ever-faithful God,*
> *keep us faithful.*

Amen.

Family Spiritual Nutrition

While his kindergarten class tramped around the local zoo, two by two, a little boy squeezed his teacher's hand (she was his field-trip buddy for the day), looked up into the bright blue spring sky and said, "Isn't this a beautiful day our God has made?" Later, when the surprised public schoolteacher told his parents the story, they thrilled at knowing that their five-year-old spoke so naturally about spiritual things.

Surely, that is the goal of all Christian parents—to see our children integrate their faith into daily life.

The Fifth Dimension?

While one of Carol's sons was trying to explain his Viewmaster to his dad, they discussed the meaning of the term, *three-dimensional.* "There's a fourth dimension, too—" the youngster said. "Time." Then they talked about the possibility of a fifth dimension, and he said, "I think the fifth dimension is the spiritual world—sort of."

Perhaps our relationship to God *is* the fifth dimension of life—sort of. We live not just in space and time but in another dimension—one that extends toward God.

In order to grow in that spiritual dimension, we need nourishment. Church services, Sunday school, and youth activities fill our need for corporate worship and fellowship with God's people, but we don't want to compartmentalize our lives in such a way that our kids think that spiritual things only happen in a church building or on a retreat.

Family Devotions

The subject of family devotions, however, often evokes more guilt than a sling-shot-toting kid caught near a lifeless prize rooster.

Sometimes we rush through family devotions, late for another commitment. Sometimes they become a mealtime ritual of Bible reading during which we daydream. Sometimes they're skipped altogether.

A number of the mothers in our survey said they had family devotions of one sort or another but felt their devotions weren't all they could be—especially in less structured times such as summer.

One mom says, "Our family worship exists, but it is not as consistent as I would like it to be. We have devotions together after supper, but often my husband feels hurried to get to meetings."

Another wrote, "In the summer our devotions easily drift," and still another added, "I do hope God is patient and forgiving when we fail to spend time in family devotions."

Diversity

Perhaps, as in the case of the quiet time, we need a reminder that the terms *family devotions* and *family altar,* as some people call it, are not found in Scripture. Certainly the principle of passing on spiritual truth to our offspring is scriptural, but the Bible doesn't dictate *how* we should do it. Mealtime devotions may have been most convenient for many generations because that was the time when all or most of the family was together, but this particular time is not a mandate. With today's busier schedules we may have to be more creative in finding family times for spiritual input.

The psalmist Asaph wrote,

> We *will* tell the next generation the praiseworthy deeds of the Lord, his power, and the wonders he has done . . . so the next generation would know them, even the children yet to be born, and they in turn would tell their children. Then they would put their trust in God and would not forget his deeds but would keep his commands. (Psalm 78:4, 6–7, emphasis ours)

The rest of the psalm goes on to delineate many of the wonderful things God has graciously done for his people in spite of the fact that we have not always been faithful to Him.

The principle of passing on spiritual truth from one generation to the next is there, but we have a great deal of flexibility in the *how* department. Because of the differences in family personalities and schedules, each family will need to find what works best for them. Single-parent families, two-career families, and families in which one parent is a believer and the other has no interest in spiritual things will probably devise different practices for spiritual nourishment than Christian families in which Dad works forty hours a week and Mom stays home. And even among the latter, different personalities will make different choices.

The mother of a five-year-old and a nine-year-old says, "Our family worship is around the dinner table with special emphasis on their Sunday school papers and the activities found in those."

Another mom says, "I bought a devotional·for each one of the kids, and one for my husband and me. I try to spend time on these after dinner with one child each night."

A third mother reads a story from the Bible with her kids at lunch and prays with them about family concerns, and then her husband leads supper-time devotions.

Later in the evening is better for another mom: "At bedtime I read a Bible story to my two youngest and pray with them. I encourage my three older children to have personal devotions at bedtime as my husband and I do."

Some families use brief readings from devotional booklets (See Appendix D), others read directly from the Scriptures, and some use a combination of the two and vary their format. A mother of five says, "One summer we studied the book of Mark together, using a notebook. The kids did a chapter on Sunday afternoon, and that was the basis for lunchtime devotions."

Other families use drama, music, or even games to make spiritual truths vital and exciting. One mother says, "Some summers we have tried using a few Bible trivia questions at every meal."

Some parents are not comfortable with the traditional, formal approach of family devotions—prayer and Bible reading after a meal. In one family in which the children attend a very conservative Christian school, the kids strongly resisted formal devotions at home. "We get Scripture all day long at school," one of the kids said. "Can't we have a break?"

Knowing the child was not saying this in disrespect of Scripture, the parents realized that they needed to find other ways of passing along the particular spiritual truths they wanted to make sure their children knew, while at the same time not alienating their children by "cramming Scripture down their throats."

They did not abandon prayer or Bible reading altogether. They prayed with the children in the mornings, at mealtimes, and at bedtime. And Scripture and scriptural principles were woven into daily activities.

They adopted the Deuteronomy 6 approach:

> Be careful to obey . . . Love the Lord your God with all your heart and with all your soul and with all your strength. These commandments that I give you today are to be upon your hearts. *Impress them on your children.* Talk about them when you sit at home and when you walk along the road, when you lie down and when you get up." (Deuteronomy 6:3, 5–7, emphasis ours)

When walking with the kids in the woods, these parents talked about the great God who must be extremely smart to have made all the various kinds of trees, plants, and animals. They talked about how much God loves us—that He would give us all these beautiful things to enjoy.

When the children were having trouble getting along because of selfishness, they talked about "each esteeming the other better than himself" (Philippians 2:3).

When one of the children was rushed to the hospital with

cuts from a broken window, they talked about God's loving care in preventing a more serious injury.

They also kept Christian music playing all the time and bought children's tapes of Scripture songs and Christian themes, which the kids listened to over and over again. Spiritual values and teachings became an integral part of their lives.

What Are We to Teach?

The two key concepts in the Deuteronomy portion of Scripture cited above are to obey God and to love God. Jesus taught that obeying is the natural result of loving. He said, "If anyone loves me, he will obey my teaching . . . He who does not love me will not obey my teaching" (John 14:23–24). The more we teach our children about His awesome creation, the good things He has done for us personally, and His interest in every detail of our lives, the more likely our children will learn to obey His Word. It is always more enjoyable to do things for people we love.

And if we teach our children to love God first, we can avoid the legalism and rigidness that often drives kids away rather than attracts them to spiritual things. If we can show our children that the rules God has laid down for us are for our own good, because of His love for us, they may be less likely to chafe under them.

When Are We to Teach?

Deuteronomy mentions four specific situations in which we can impress spiritual truth on our children—when we sit at home, when we walk [or drive] along the road, when we lie down, and when we get up. What God is saying here is: *Do it anytime, anywhere. Make it a natural part of your life.*

The Deuteronomy 6 approach is a moment-by-moment integration of spiritual concepts with daily living. If we have had our "devotions" at mealtime or bedtime, there is the danger of feeling we have discharged our spiritual responsibility. But if those devotions are forced, dull, mechanical, or done simply because Christian families are *supposed* to have devotions together, the picture of God and His ways that we have given our children may be quite the opposite of what we intend. And by feeling we have discharged our responsibility, we may pass up some of the richest opportunities for spiritual teaching in the everyday events of life.

Also, if the only time we talk about how our faith affects our lives is at the family devotion time, spiritual things can become compartmentalized—separate from life.

Bumping Into God . . .

In their book *Together at Home,* Dean and Grace Merrill share some of their secrets:

> We mix the "secular" with the "sacred," the "fun" with the "religious," so kids don't know the difference. That is intentional. We don't want our kids putting God in a Sunday/church box. We want them bumping into God every time they turn around, in the midst of ordinary living. That way God will stay a normal, here-and-now part of their lives into adulthood.[1]

The Merrills see the fairly recent practice of a weekly "family night" as an alternative to daily family devotions in which inconsistency spawns guilt. And guilt often leads to giving up the practice altogether. Their book is stuffed full of good ideas for nurturing our kids' faith through nitty-gritty "that's-life" experiences, not just a weekly family time. They use fun chapter titles such as: "Pig-out Prevention," "The Pinocchio Principle: Lying," and "If You Controlled the Checkbook: Teaching about Finances."

More Structured Times

Still, some families have made the more structured family devotions a habit. It works for them—at least most of the time. They feel more comfortable planning a regular time in order to avoid the all-too-common pitfall of not having much devotional time at all with their kids.

Radio broadcaster and author Harold Sala says, "One of the most important [secrets to successful family devotions] is to bring our children into this time together as equals and fellow participants—not as kids who are going to get an injection of Bible as a kind of spiritual vitamin B."[2]

Some families let their kids take turns leading the devotions once a week. Others make assignments such as a scripture portion to read and/or memorize, and then the family discusses its personal application during their devotional time together.

One of the finest books on making family devotions interesting and relevant is Mary White's *Successful Family Devotions*. The cover blurb says, "For families who can't sit still for formal family devotions, here's a natural way to teach your kids spiritual truth—and let them enjoy it!"[3] This book gives practical suggestions for adding fun and variety to family devotions as well as many ideas for integrating the spiritual with the secular in everything from manners to fashion to social issues.

The author also gives specific recommendations for children at different ages (tots, tweens, and teens) and appropriate ideas for special occasions (weddings, birthdays, Thanksgiving, Easter, Christmas, Fourth of July). The final chapter cites five keys to continuing: conviction, planning, brevity, variety, and flexibility.

Mary White says, "Family devotions can be the greatest investment you will make in your children . . . God will give you the will and discipline needed to lead and to feed your children a balanced diet of spiritual food."[4]

We have included other family devotions resources in Appendix D, but whatever methods a family decides to use to feed themselves spiritually, balanced nutrition is important.

The Two Basic Spiritual Food Groups

Just as we need a balanced diet from the four basic food groups for our physical well-being, we also need a balanced diet from the two basic spiritual food groups for our *spiritual* well-being. They are: Scripture and prayer.

Scripture

The world constantly bombards our minds with messages it wants us to hear:

- You can have anything you want today (and pay later).
- You have to look, smell, and act a certain way to be accepted.
- Pre-marital and extra-marital sex are just part of life.

Therefore, we need frequent exposure to God's thoughts and His messages. He says, "My thoughts are not your thoughts, neither are your ways my ways" (Isaiah 55:8). The best means for us to learn His ways is to read His words, meditate on them, and memorize them—in whatever ways we find workable in our family situation.

Reading—Probably one of the quickest ways to turn our kids off to spiritual things is to open the Bible at random after dinner when their friends are sitting on the front porch, waiting to play with them, and to begin reading in "hallowed" tones for an interminable period of time from a version they can't understand. And if we just leave the words we've read hanging there—no commentary, no discussion—we can be sure that we have not whetted their appetite for more.

The more we relate what we read to what's going on in the world, in our community, in their classrooms, and in their relationships with their friends, the more ownership they will have of their Christian faith and the more exciting it will be to them.

It also helps to share how scriptural principles may have influenced the way we handled a situation in our work or relationships during the day—or to confess the times we blew it: We knew God wouldn't be pleased if we kept the extra change the grocery store clerk erroneously gave us, but we were in a hurry. . . . And now we have to make a special trip back to the store to make things right. Talking openly about how God's guidelines affect the way we live helps our kids see how they can let Scripture mold their lives as well.

Mary White says, "In Christian homes the words of God should be discussed and repeated as naturally and as often as we would comment on the weather, but with infinitely more importance. Talking of spiritual things should be vital, but not stilted; natural, but not frivolous; frequent, but not tedious."[5]

How do we avoid being tedious in our Scripture reading?

Some families take turns, each reading a verse of the selected portion and then discussing it. Others ask each of the kids to read the same verse from a different translation or paraphrase, and then they all talk about the insights the various wordings give.

Memorization—The times when the kids are on a break from school are some of the best times for Scripture memorization, thanks to a reprieve from schoolwork pressure. Some families like a structured system like that of the Navigators or Bible Memory Association. (See Appendix D for details and addresses.)

Other families like to tailor their memory activities to the particular needs, interests, and abilities of their families. Some prefer memorizing directly from their Bibles during a devotional time while others have their kids write verses on 3 × 5 cards, which they can take with them when they climb up a tree by themselves or find a quiet spot by a stream or in the attic.

One mom says, "My children memorize a proverb a week. I post it on the refrigerator, and they recite it at evening devotions."

Other families may use a topical approach, covering such areas as salvation, assurance, God's character, and Christian growth.

Plan of salvation—A group of verses such as the following that tell how a person can come to faith in Christ is a wonderful foundation to memorize:

- *God loves us*—John 3:16—"For God so loved the world that he gave his one and only Son, that whoever believes in him shall not perish but have eternal life."
- *We have all sinned*—Romans 3:23—"For all have sinned and fall short of the glory of God."
- *Sin separates us from God*—Romans 6:23a—"For the wages of sin is death . . ."
- *God offers us eternal life as a free gift*—Romans 6:23b—"but the gift of God is eternal life in Christ Jesus our Lord."
- *If we accept Him, we become His children*—John 1:12—"To all who received him, to those who believed in his name, he gave the right to become children of God."
- *We can be sure we have eternal life*—1 John 5:13—"I write

these things to you who believe in the name of the Son of God so that you may *know* that you have eternal life" (emphasis ours).

These verses can speak to our kids' hearts if they haven't yet received Christ as their Savior. And they can be useful tools in helping them lead their friends to the Lord.

Longer passages—Dean and Grace Merrill believe in stretching our kids. They say, "The last couple of summers we've challenged our children to master a longer passage: an entire psalm or other classic text, such as Philippians 2:5–16, James 1:1–12, John 14, or a chapter of the Sermon on the Mount (Matthew 5–7)."[6] They offered rewards and found that the kids memorized the material and claimed their prizes by the end of June.

"Children this age have ink-blotter brains that are more than equal to mountainous-sounding tasks," the Merrills continue. "They love the challenge, followed by the satisfaction of being able to recite a whole section of God's Word."[7]

Some families may ask the kids to memorize throughout the entire summer while others may try a blitz approach, asking each child in a specified period of time to memorize as many verses as they are years old. Others may feel that the verses their kids are assigned through their Christian school, church clubs such as AWANA, or their Sunday-school program provide an adequate challenge.

Family times can also be a good time to teach kids how to use a concordance and other reference works. Then kids could be assigned verses to learn that have a particular word in them, such as *sheep* or *time*.

The differences in family style, personalities, and temperaments often determine whether a family just picks a few verses they want their kids to grasp during the summer or whether they have a more ambitious plan.

Tip: If the kids say they can't memorize at all, ask them their best friend's telephone number.

Music—Setting a portion of Scripture to music can be a fun experience for the kids and make memorization easier. At one time the Ellises made up a little tune for each of their kids' memory verses. A simple melody and repetition carved the Scripture into the children's memory.

Suiting style of music to the words also helps. For instance, the tune for Romans 6:23 began slowly in a minor key to express "For the wages of sin is death," and then picked up tempo and changed to a major key as they sang, "but the gift of God is eternal life, through Jesus Christ our Lord" (KJV). They recorded these verses onto a cassette for future reference, and the kids enjoyed playing their verse songs from time to time.

God's truth can also make inroads into our lives through hymns. Many of the older hymns, especially, are either based directly on Scripture or expand on a biblical phrase or principle. "O God Our Help in Ages Past" is a beautiful reminder of Psalm 90. "Praise the Lord! Ye Heavens Adore Him" majestically interprets Psalm 148. And who hasn't been uplifted by singing "Great Is Thy Faithfulness" (Lamentations 3:22–23).

There are many avenues for teaching God's truth through music if we remain alert. God promises us that His Word will not return to Him void, and when we set scriptural principles to music, they ride a freeway to the heart.

Some of the moms we surveyed used music for spiritual nourishment, too. One mom said, "On Sundays we gather around the piano, pull out our instruments, and play and sing Christian songs." Another said, "I play a selection of Christian music each morning during my piano practice time to set a good tone for the kids as they wake up." Still another said, "I bought some new 'Kids Praise' tapes at the Christian bookstore for all of us to enjoy this summer."

Prayer

Prayer is an opportunity for us to express our personal feelings, our frustrations, and our needs to God, but we miss out on a great deal if that's the *only* type of praying we do.

Family matters—Joyce and her husband, in trying to share the "parenting" load when the kids were small, arranged for Mom to get the kids up in the morning and for Dad to put them to bed, praying with each child individually at night. When they began school, Mom prayed with each one just before they went out the door, asking God to protect, guide, and help them show His love to those around them.

The practice became a habit, and even on days when Mom wasn't feeling well and slept in, the kids came into her room and sat on the edge of her bed while she prayed with them. She has been pleasantly surprised that her high-schoolers still ask her to pray with them before they leave in the mornings.

There are many opportunities to pray with our kids in all types of situations.

When we have lost our way on a family vacation, we can pull over to the side of the road and ask the Lord to help us find the right road (and then thank Him afterward, even if, much to our husbands' consternation, God has to use a gas station attendant or other total stranger to point us in the right direction).

When our finances are already tight and we're hit with an unexpected car-repair bill, we may be sitting at the table with the family, trying to figure out where to tighten our belts one more notch without it pinching too much. Right there we can pray for God's help in meeting this need (and then thank Him afterward when He provides some extra funds from an unexpected source or shows us some area that we could cut without harming the family's welfare).

When our kids come home upset because their best friend has threatened never to speak to them again, we can sit down and pray that the Lord will heal the hurt and restore the relationship (and then thank the Lord afterward when they are playing happily again—often the very next day).

"Take it to the Lord in prayer," says the old gospel song. And that is our privilege—to take all our family's concerns and needs to Him. When the world teaches us to be totally independent and self-sufficient, praying with our kids is a way of acknowledging our constant *dependence* upon God.

If a family is involved in a prayer chain and receives a call to pray, or if the family receives bad news about a friend or relative, that phone call provides an excellent opportunity to pray with your children.

When Joyce's father had a serious setback a few hours after open-heart surgery, she called some friends to ask them to pray. She was deeply moved the next day, after the danger was past, when those friends said that after her call, the whole family stopped what they were doing, gathered in the living room, and prayed for her dad.

Many parents encourage their children to pray aloud, taking turns at meals and/or devotions, and praying at bedtime or times of family concern.

Also, the possibilities for prayers of thanksgiving and praise are endless—the salvation of a friend, a rainbow after a storm, a brilliant sunset, a narrow escape from an accident, evidence of spiritual growth, a missing item found.

Remembering others—Sometimes, we tend to be a little too nearsighted in our prayers. But family prayer times can stretch our vision beyond our own family, such as praying for friends and relatives who don't yet know the Lord, praying for missionaries, and praying for church and government leaders.

The more specific we can be in helping our children visualize what we're praying for, the better. Let's face it. Sitting quietly with our eyes closed can get rather boring unless we have something to focus on. "God, bless our leaders in government" isn't as meaningful as "God, please help our President and Congress make the right decision regarding _____ (fill in some issue that is currently in the news)." Apart from the benefit to our children, it is always better to pray specifically anyway. Specific prayers get specific answers.

"God bless all the missionaries" isn't as visual to a child as "God, please help Mr. Swanson as he and his Costa Rican co-workers try to build a bigger church to hold all the people who have come to Christ in the past year."

Some families use a photo album of missionaries they have met and other special friends they pray for regularly. Others use prayer directories from their local church or denomination with pictures and information about various missionaries. They pray for one person or one couple each day or each week. Some families adopt one missionary family that they can get to know personally, correspond with, and pray for often.

One mother we surveyed told about her family's pledge to pray regularly for a Wycliffe Bible translator. She says, "Wycliffe has a list of thousands of language groups that do not have any portion of Scripture in their language or even any translators to begin the work. They give the name of a tribe to prayer partners who request it, and they send along information about the tribe. My husband and I prayed for a group for several years, and now two translators are there. Each of our three daughters also has the name of a tribe for whom to pray. They have a reminder card, they learn some geography, and they pray daily."

Another mom says, "Each evening we have a different prayer topic—such as missionaries, family, or church needs."

We certainly won't be able to do all of the things suggested here. We may try different approaches at times for variety. But in whatever ways we find to turn our attention heavenward through prayer, God will strengthen our bond with Him and thereby strengthen the faith of both parents and children.

Glimmers of Light

Often we focus on the struggles we have with our kids, their seeming disinterest in spiritual things, and their inability to get along with one another. But just one little glimmer of light— some tiny evidence of spiritual growth in our kids—can make up for many of the darker days.

One of the moms in our survey said, "Yesterday I overheard the girls talking about how lonely Aunt Ella is after Aunt Bessie died (two elderly aunts who lived together). Our five-year-old said, 'That's why we need to pray for her.' "

Carol looks back fondly on the time one of her sons said, "I prayed for a nice day for our picnic today, and God sent it!" and the time one of them remained silent during bedtime prayers, then said shyly, "I asked God to forgive me for losing my temper tonight."

We'll take those little glimmers of light anytime!

Alertness

The most important thing about spiritual times with our families is not when, how often, or what we do in those times but rather that we remain alert for opportunities to share spiritual truth in an interesting, practical way, to "tell the next generation the praiseworthy deeds of the Lord, his power, and the wonders he has done . . . so the next generation would know them, even the children yet to be born, and they in turn would tell their children. Then they would put their trust in God" (Psalm 78:4, 6–7).

———————— *Looking Up* ————————

Lord of the Living Word,
    So live in our hearts
    and in our daily actions
    that our children
    will be excited about You,
    someday exciting their own children
    about Your awesome ways!
    Make our joy contagious, Lord.

                                                 Amen.

◊ **10** ◊

"What Can I Do Now, Mom?"

The school year ended at 3:00 Wednesday afternoon, and at 10:30 the next morning, a little boy slumped into a chair in the kitchen and said, "Mom, I'm bored. There's nothing to do."

He hadn't even made it twenty-four hours without encountering boredom!

When our kids say they're bored, we sometimes react with:

Guilt: "I'm creating a dull environment for my children."

Anger: "All the options in the world around you, and you're bored? When I was a kid, I didn't have half the opportunities you have."

Helplessness: "There's nothing I can do about it. No matter what I suggest, you'll turn up your nose at it anyway."

In trying to relieve their children's boredom, some of the moms we surveyed use a scatter-gun approach. They said, "First I try _____, then I try _____, and if that doesn't work, I try _____. The way they filled in those blanks varied widely.

On the other hand, some moms said that they wouldn't even

allow the word *bored* to be uttered in their houses. Their children knew that if they said they were bored, they were automatically assigned extra chores.

Psychologist and author Dr. Dan Kiley sees a number of connections between work and boredom. For example, he suggests assigning "boring chores" when we want to discipline our children for misconduct. He sees boredom as one of the most effective punishments we can create for children—they hate to be bored.

But Dr. Kiley also advocates regular, daily chores for kids as a way of teaching them *how to handle boredom.* "When chores become habitual," he says, "a child has an easier time adjusting to other boring times."[1]

What Is Boredom?

By dictionary definition, boredom is a state of being restless or weary because an event is uninteresting.

But is that all there is to it? Most kids haven't read the dictionary definition. What do *they* mean when they say they are bored?

For an answer, Carol consulted an expert on boredom, her thirteen-year-old son. "Last summer when you said you were bored, what did you mean by that?" she asked.

Her son thought a moment. "I meant that I wanted to do something that you wouldn't let me do," he replied.

New insight dawned. "Was that always what you meant?" Carol probed.

"No, sometimes I meant I had a lot of energy and didn't know what to do with it. I needed to use it up."

"Okay, anything else?"

"Sometimes I just felt restless and tired, and I didn't really know why. Nothing seemed interesting."

This little interview painted a different picture of boredom. At least for some kids, boredom is a three-headed monster!

- *Parental punishment.* "You won't let me bike to town in the heat, and now it's your fault that I have nothing interesting to do."

- *Seeking suggestions.* "I can't think of anything to do. Do you have any ideas?"
- *Restless fatigue.* "I want to do something, but I don't have any energy."

Perhaps this bit of wisdom explains the scatter-gun approach of many moms. We may be trying to meet one need when that's not the problem area. So by trial and error, we keep making suggestions, hoping we'll find out what will relieve the type of boredom our kids are experiencing *this* time.

We don't necessarily have to make our kids lie down on our mental "psychiatrist's couch" and figure out which of boredom's three ugly heads is rearing up at this moment. But an awareness of the various factors might help us ask specific questions in order to make appropriate suggestions.

If our children are trying to penalize us, we could suggest a visit to Mars and they would reject it. When they need to channel energy, they would readily climb aboard the spaceship. The restless fatigue element is probably the hardest to combat. Those two elements are warring inside. Restlessness makes the kids want activity, but their weariness causes them to reject any suggestion. At that point, a nap may be one of the best solutions.

Need for Variety

A Minnesota piano teacher suggests another cause of boredom: overexposure. When her grade-school piano pupils tell her that a piece is boring, she asks how much they have practiced it. Usually, if the students are honest, they'll answer, "Not very much." She tells them they *can't* be bored with the piece then. They've barely become acquainted with it. If they had practiced it over and over to the point of overexposure, then they could legitimately claim boredom.

Overexposure *can* make almost anything seem boring—playing the same game too often or too long, watching TV too long, playing with the same friends too long, even reading too long. Providing variety can head off some of the normal boredom our kids face.

Many mothers provide variety through a balance of work

and play. Either can get boring if the kids do it for too long at a time—even play.

One of the mothers who didn't allow the word *bored* in her house had her children make a list of things they enjoyed doing, and they posted the list on the refrigerator door. When the kids felt bored, they could consult the list to remind themselves of games, puzzles, toys, tapes, or other activities they may have forgotten.

One year, before school let out, an Iowa mother of two planned ahead and prepared an activity file. She says, "I sat down for a few evenings and wrote up activity options on file cards. I took some suggestions from *Childcraft*, which has many ideas, but sometimes children find it more difficult to select them from the book. When the kids need something to do, they may either pull a card from their age-appropriate file or flip through and find something that appeals to them."

Here are some samples from her activity file:

- Use seashells to make animals or designs.
- Compose a tune on the piano. Put words to it.
- Make a jigsaw puzzle by pasting a picture to tagboard or cardboard and cutting it up. Don't cut the pieces too small! Variation: Before cutting, write a letter on the back side of the puzzle and then cut and mail the pieces to a friend.
- Write a story in picture language. Ask someone to read it.
- Start a diary. Write at least one interesting thing that happens each day.
- Find out: What is an anemometer? Who was William Tell? Where does the Painted Desert get its name?
- Have a picnic for your dolls and stuffed animals.
- Lie on a blanket outside. Look at the clouds. What shapes do you see?
- Write a letter or card to your teacher. Tell her what you are doing this summer.
- Catch an insect. Look at it through a magnifying glass. Draw its face.

(For additional activities see Chapter 11.)

A Kentucky mother of three had a similar idea. She wrote her activity suggestions on cards and put them in a box that their family named "the bored box." The child pulls a card from the box and then has a choice—to do what the card says or to quit complaining about being bored.

In an article titled, "Mommy, I'm Bored," Melissa Bregenzer suggests a number of other strategies for preventing boredom. Perhaps the most notable of these is to "Get kids involved in long-term projects: Chart the weather. Make a gauge to measure rainfall, note wind directions . . . Encourage them to befriend a neighbor who would welcome company . . . prompt older kids to script a movie and videotape it, complete with costumes."[2]

One group of neighborhood kids, most of whom were Christians, worked all summer writing, staging, and rehearsing a play with a Christian theme, which they performed in August for their parents and others in the neighborhood. Parents provided some help with props, costumes, and scenery, but the kids did most of the work themselves. It kept them busy, developed their creativity, and provided hours of fun as well as a Christian testimony to the neighborhood.

Anticipation

Some of the boredom of summer can be alleviated by giving the kids something to look forward to. Whether it's weekly, biweekly, or even monthly, a special outing planned in advance can break the monotony of trying to think up things to do every day.

Even short-term promises can be effective. If mom is busy cleaning the kitchen and the kids are having trouble staying busy, Mom might offer to play a game with them at a specified time if they can occupy themselves until then or if they help her finish more quickly so that she can play with them. Short games work well for this. One mom says, "I keep my eye out for good board games which can be finished in fifteen to twenty minutes."

Time Alone With One Parent

Sometimes a boredom cry might indicate a child's need for personal time with one or both parents. Consistent with Murphy's Law, often the time that they need personal attention is the time when we are least able to give it—when we're in the middle of fixing dinner, while we're filling out our tax forms— hours or minutes before the extension deadline—or during a phone call.

If it's possible to bring them into our situation, such as asking them to stir the white sauce while we prepare the toast baskets or letting them say hello to whomever we are talking to on the phone (when appropriate), this is a good way to affirm how important our children are to us. But if we can't realistically stop what we're doing at that moment or can't ask them to help in such things as computing the depreciation on a home-business expense, sometimes a loving touch (a hug or squeezing their hand) and a promise to do something with them alone as soon as we get to a stopping point will also satisfy them.

We don't have to feel guilty if we can't quit what we're doing *every time* our kids want our attention. They also need to learn that the world does not revolve around them.

Spending some personal time with each of our kids regularly can often *prevent* some of their boredom, too.

Reaching Out

Sometimes when our kids are bored, we can help them channel their energy into doing things for others. If there is an elderly widow or widower in your neighborhood or church family, you might want to encourage the kids to make some cookies, a scrapbook (see Chapter 11 for ideas), or some other meaningful gift for that person. Then make the presentation of their gift a special event. If we remind our children that people who live alone may often become bored, too, we may help our kids to stop focusing on themselves.

Reading

According to the moms we surveyed, one of their most common responses to boredom complaints was, "Go read" or "Let's read." We discussed this subject in more detail in Chapter 9, but it bears repeating that reading is a wonderful way for kids to occupy their time. And somehow it can be a little more fun if the kids are allowed to climb a tree or find some other "dreamy" spot, such as a fallen tree in the woods, or a lake, river, stream, or ocean, where they can escape into the wonderful world of books. (For recommended reading list, see Appendix D.)

Change of Pace

When every day seems just like the one before, sometimes our kids (and their moms) just need a break. One mother says that on days like that, "I take them for ice cream cones or uptown just to get away for a short time. Sometimes I suggest they invite friends to come over or to go swimming with them."

This brings up another area that for some moms is a struggle.

The Role of Playmates

While neighborhood friends often provide lots of opportunities for our kids to play (as well as relief from boredom), they also bring some frustrations.

The Van Klompenburgs' two living situations pointed out a few reasons why some mothers struggle with the role of neighborhood playmates. Carol remembers what it was like living on a cul-de-sac where the grade-school children outnumbered the adults. Backyards were filled with swing sets, sandboxes, and bodies in motion. Sometimes the kids seemed to move in herds.

They pushed each other on the swings, built sand castles together, and played hide-and-seek across the yards. Neighborhood moms freely shared popsicles on a hot summer day.

But sometimes the kids formed name-calling cliques, threw sand in one another's eyes, or got hurt from carelessness or dangerous stunts—like the time a boy broke his arm playing Superman off the Van Klompenburg swing set.

Three years ago Carol's family moved to the country, lured by the memories Carol and her husband had of growing up on farms. But "peace and quiet" can be a mixed blessing.

On days when the three children play together in their sandbox, take turns on their huge tire swing, and play tag around the house together, Carol loves it. When they grow restless and bored with the company of siblings only, fight over the swing, and knock down one another's sand castles, her love for the country falters. On days that boredom sets in, she often imports playmates—some from the old neighborhood.

No living situation is perfect. Many mothers struggle with a balance between their kids' herd activity and loneliness. Playmates can make our kids' lives more enjoyable and prevent boredom, but playmates can also frustrate mothers.

Playmate Joys

A Texas mother of two says, "As long as their friends respect our lifestyle, we encourage our kids to spend time with friends. Kids can be a joy—good teaching tools in getting to know ourselves and observing character qualities in others. Friends can also rub off some of our rough edges."

Playmates from families with personalities different from our own also bring ideas, games, and activities from their background that can enhance *our* children's play and broaden their world.

Playmate Frustrations

But the joys often fade when frustrations lead to legitimate complaints:

A South Dakota mother of three said, "My five-year-old spent many hours at a neighbor's house at the beginning of summer until I realized he was watching rock videos and hearing a lot of bad language from his playmate's older brother."

A Michigan mom wrote, "Sometimes I have up to twelve children in our yard. Not all are Christians, and sometimes there is foul language and bullying. I worry about my children absorbing values we don't promote."

And a mother of five from New Mexico said, "It is extremely frustrating to feel that the rules of our family are good and fair and yet have difficulty enforcing them because other kids have another set of standards contrary to ours."

Because families differ in their rules and standards—especially when some aren't Christians—we may need to come to some agreements with our neighbors and with our own children.

Playmate Guidelines

Many of the mothers we surveyed spelled out a number of guidelines that helped keep the peace when the kids were home:

- Children who wish to play in our house or yard will obey our rules.
- If we aren't comfortable with the activities and behavior in the home of one of our children's friends, we may ask our kids to play with that friend only at our home under our supervision.
- If there are more than one or two neighbor children who want to play together, we encourage them to play outside unless it is very hot. Then we send them to the basement.
- No neighbor children are allowed inside the house unless the host parents say it's okay.
- We set time limits. If our kids ask permission for a friend to play at our house and we agree, we also tell them how long the friend may stay.
- Neighbor children are not allowed to play in our yard or ring our doorbell during the dinner hour.
- If our children are not getting along with neighbor children, we reserve the right to send the neighbor kids home.

All of these ideas may not apply to everyone, and some families will have other rules, but we can pick and choose those that might be useful in our family situations. With a few guidelines, we can quiet some of our fears and frustrations as mothers, and our children can better enjoy playing with their friends— hopefully experiencing less boredom.

Whose Responsibility?

Even if our kids had all the friends in the world, they would still be bored sometimes. Boredom is a common problem for many people of all ages—not just children. Each year there are a number of magazine articles published that address boredom as it relates to such areas as the workplace, marriage, teen activities, exercise, and the elderly.

Ultimately, we might ask why *we* take responsibility for our kids' boredom?

Although it may be depressing first thing in the morning to hear a kid ask, "What are we going to do today that's special?" some moms throw the ball back into their child's court and say, "I don't know. What *are* you going to do today that's special?"

Howard Hendricks says,

> If you are always doing everything for your child, you are conditioning her to expect constant personal involvement. You can mother and father a child to the point that she grows up thinking she's the center of the universe. Then, the minute Mom or Dad leaves the room, the child becomes inadequate.
>
> Neither abandoning a child to the TV set nor taking the responsibility for your child's amusement is wholesome. Your child needs to learn to be able to entertain herself and use time alone creatively.[3]

Boredom can plague anyone at any time. Our kids won't always have us standing over their shoulders giving them suggestions. We may provide them with some ideas from time to time, but one mom says, "I refuse to feel guilty about my kids' boredom. God has given me the responsibility of preparing them for life, and boredom, at times, is part of it."

——————— *Looking Up* ———————

Life-giving Lord,
   You promised us
   abundant life
   in Christ.
   Teach us
   to abide in You
   that we may enjoy it
   ourselves
   and model it
   for our children.

Amen.

◊ **11** ◊

Inside, Outside, All About the Town

For many of us, summer activity books tend to be guilt factories. We look at all the projects and activities so carefully explained and beautifully illustrated, and all we can think about is the mess we'll have to clean up afterward and the additional clutter of all these precious creations we don't dare throw out because our children made them.

Some of the projects in those books are complicated; others are too easy and wouldn't interest our kids, anyway. Most require adult supervision. So we sigh, feel guilty that we aren't providing our children enough creative outlets, and envy the Supermom who surely does an indoor project with her children every morning, and an outdoor one each afternoon.

Then we remind ourselves that Supermom is a myth.

Going Overboard

As we mentioned earlier, we do not believe that a mother has to be the activities director on the cruise ship of life, keeping kids supplied with things to do every waking moment.

In fact, we may need to be careful that we aren't over-scheduling our kids' lives. If we enroll them in so many organized sports, lessons, and activities that we can hardly transport them from one event to the other without getting out of breath, we might want to take a look at our schedules and motives.

Could we be using activities as a baby-sitter? Could we be pushing our kids in order to create superkids? Could we be trying to make ourselves look good? Could our "pushing" make our kids feel we love them for their performance rather than for themselves?

Some experts are expressing concern about the increasing number of Type-A children our society is producing. Paul Bracke, an Oakland psychologist who has been involved in a Stanford University study of Type-A behavior in children says, "When you see 10-year-olds with cardiovascular stress symptoms, that says something about the way we live. . . . It's not healthy for adults, and it's not good for children, either."[1]

And when we consider the amount of money some of us sink into programs and activities to "keep our kids busy," we may want to ask ourselves if that is the best stewardship of our finances. We need to find balance. We want to develop our kids' talents to help them reach their full potential, but can we afford to overdo it?

After watching the Olympics with her family, Minneapolis author Carole K. Halmrast wrote an opinion article called, "Why We Aren't Going for the Gold." After discussing her own children's abilities, which might have Olympic potential if everyone else in the family sacrificed everything for that one, she says,

> Where do you draw the line? How does a parent set priorities, decide which child gets what, which talent will be pushed to what limit? Is it even possible for everyone to be developed to the fullest? Can we all be champions?
>
> Hardly. Realistically, for just one of my children to reach fullest flower means that another would barely bud, much less bloom. There simply aren't enough hours in the day to nurture each child's possible talents to the ultimate peak.[2]

Halmrast votes for letting all our kids develop their talents without pushing. "Perhaps none of us will ever *excel* in anything, but oh, boy, will we ever be good!" she says. "And maybe, just maybe, that's good enough."[3]

In our society's push for excellence, we may be pushing our

kids too hard, rather than letting them just play and enjoy their childhood.

"If I had it to do all over again," one mother says, "I probably wouldn't schedule so much structure into my kids' lives. I'd just let them be kids."

Cutting Costs

One of the best gifts we can give our kids is the ability to enjoy themselves without spending money. Schools and even many churches aren't teaching that. With several children in a family, field trips and church club activities can quickly break a family's budget. Yes, it's fun to go miniature golfing, bowling, and roller or ice skating at an indoor rink, but these can be the occasional treat rather than the steady diet of the school, church, and family activity program. There are so many fun things for kids to do that cost little or nothing. Many are listed later in this chapter.

A Place for Activities

In this book we have tried to present more principles and ideas than specific activities, knowing that the personalities and interests of children (and parents) differ a great deal. But we know that some moms are always looking for something new, fun, and easy to do with their kids, so we've set aside this chapter for a number of ideas and activities that worked for the families we surveyed.

Inside Activities

Interestingly, according to the moms we heard from, kids most enjoyed the "ordinary" things: coloring, drawing, playing with *Lego* or other building blocks, making story books, reading, looking through family pictures, playing house, playing school, playing dress-up with Mom's and Dad's cast-off clothing, playing piano, and playing board games—*Monopoly, Scrabble, Clue,* Checkers (the list is endless).

Both kids and moms came up with other creative, fun, and

often educational ideas for keeping busy. Some are common, but they might be possibilities you had forgotten about.

We doubt that anyone—even Supermom—could do them all, nor would a person want to. So again we encourage you to pick and choose ideas that might be fun for you and your kids for an occasional "something different."

Many parents recommend keeping on hand plenty of art supplies, such as paper, pencils, crayons, markers, colored chalk, water colors, glue, scissors, and tape.

One father, a college professor who is often home when his grade-schoolers are, says his children spend much of their free time drawing, coloring, and being creative with these simple art supplies.

If the kids go through a lot of paper, some moms encourage their children to "recycle" by using the backs of flyers and notes sent home from school, blank newsprint from the neighborhood paper carrier, and discarded computer paper.

Parents enjoy seeing their children's creative handiwork. The only problem is where to put it all. The refrigerator door can only hold so many pictures of rainbows, houses flanked by trees, and stick-people family portraits.

At one time the Ellises lived in a house that had a long hallway perfect for an art gallery. The kids chose the best of their artwork that they wanted to save, and Mom put it up. Periodically, new works of art replaced older ones, and some were saved for special memories.

Other moms use bulletin boards, let their kids hang their artwork in their rooms, or preserve it between two layers of clear *Con-tact* paper for mealtime placemats.

One mom says she always keeps paper, markers, activity books, and pillows in the car so that they're ready anytime for an outing, and the kids always have something to do.

Here are some other ideas:

Make scrapbooks for your family or to give away. Keep scrapbooks for the family holding programs from band or choir concerts, drama productions, or other special events in which the kids have participated, as well as ribbons, awards, certificates, and photos.

Scrapbooks to give away are also fun to make. Let the kids

cut from magazines and calendars pretty pictures of mountains, waterfalls, flowers, animals, etc. Paste or glue onto a scrapbook page, and find an appropriate Scripture verse to go with it. Cut these from page-a-day Scripture-verse calendars, or have the kids write or print out the verses. If they've learned calligraphy in school (or want to learn) this would be a good place to use it.

Make personalized greeting cards out of construction paper by gluing on such things as photos or pictures from old greeting cards, rickrack, lace, yarn, or other odds and ends. Print or type inside greeting.

Create air tents. If you have central air conditioning with floor vents, take an old sheet and place it over the register. Secure the edges with a row of books, allowing just enough room on one end for a person to crawl in and wait. When the air conditioner kicks in, the sheet puffs up, creating a cool place to play.

Stitch designs on burlap with pieces of yarn left over from other projects.

Make playhouses from large empty appliance boxes (often available from appliance stores or new areas of construction). Kids can cut doors and windows, tape on "shingles and siding," and decorate the interior with pictures from magazines.

Work on your family's genealogy. Get as much help as you can from relatives to construct your family tree as far back as possible. Kids can call grandparents to get much of this information. If they become really interested, you might want to include in your family vacation plans a trip to your ancestors' point of entry into the United States and do more research.

Get oral histories. Let the kids practice with relatives. Pretending to be reporters, they might ask what life was like when Grandma was little, what were her happiest memories, what was the saddest thing that ever happened to her, etc. If they become confident, they might want to do similar interviews with nursing home residents or other elderly people in the community. A tape recorder can be used for this.

Set up a stuffed-animal zoo. Using laundry baskets for cages and couch pillows for pens, put all the monkeys together in one area, all the bears in another, etc. You might want to make tickets for neighbor kids and include a puppet show and even

popcorn. Let the kids do the planning, performing, *and* cleanup.
Rearrange/redecorate. Think of new ways to arrange your
kids' rooms. You may want to wallpaper or paint, rearrange
furniture, or put up new posters and other personal touches
chosen by the kids.

Create an indoor golf course using cups lying on their sides.

Create toothpick sculptures. Using toothpicks and dried peas
as joint fasteners (soak in water for 6–8 hours first), construct
buildings, animals, or any type of sculpture desired.

Make your own Christmas presents. Teach kids to sew with
easy projects such as simple stuffed animals, needlework on
pillowcases, latch-hook pillows, etc. One family even made a
felt crèche glued onto wooden blocks.

Create a time line along a rec room wall or other available
space. On butcher paper or a roll of paper tablecloth, mark off
centuries and fill in dates interesting to your children (e.g. the
Hebrews' exodus from Egypt, the birth of Christ, fall of the
Roman Empire, birth of Helen Keller, birth of Laura Ingalls Wilder, first man to reach the moon). Let kids decorate with appropriate drawings.

Make something for a county or state fair. Even city kids can
make needlework, craft, or cooking entries. Find out how to
enter your local fair, and let the kids' imaginations suggest possible projects they might like to work on. One mom tells how
proud her five-year-old was of his second-prize ribbon for the
muffins he made for their state fair.

Outside Activities

Again, the moms we surveyed said that the activities their
kids enjoy over and over include ordinary things: riding bikes,
skateboarding, playing games, swimming, sports, hiking,
throwing frisbees, roller skating, flying kites, blowing bubbles,
and having picnics.

Here are some of their other suggestions:

Water fights. After cleaning out trigger-spray bottles or liquid-
dish-detergent bottles with squirt holes in the cap, fill them with
water and let the kids go to battle on a hot summer day.

Run through the lawn sprinkler to cool off.

Build a tree house (or clubhouse on the ground). The fun of building is as great as playing inside the structure afterward. But it does give the kids a sense of privacy, not to mention satisfaction in their accomplishment. And being part of a club is something most kids enjoy.

Play jugball. The rules are similar to baseball but the game is played with an empty plastic milk jug, a plastic bat, and shorter base paths. This is a great game for small yards.

Play tennisball—another baseball variation played with a tennis racquet and tennis ball instead of a bat and baseball or softball.

Build a backyard obstacle course. Use whatever materials the kids can find (e.g. wading pools, old tires, folding chairs, ropes). Construct an obstacle course and compete with neighbor kids, using a stopwatch to compute times.

Play water-balloon volleyball. Divide into two teams and have team members pair up. Each pair holds a towel between them, which serves as a sling for catching and throwing water balloons over a volleyball net. A team scores a point if the balloon breaks on the other side of the net. A note of caution: "You will get wet."

Variation: Give each team an old bed sheet, instructing them to hold all four sides and try to fling the water balloon over the net in a coordinated throw.

Build a table-top sandbox. To reduce the amount of sand tracked into the house, build a sandbox on top of a picnic table and make a cover for it. Take off the cover, and the kids can play in the sand without getting sandy feet. Put the top back on, and the picnic table can still be used for outdoor meals.

Take a family bike hike. Decide on a destination that's not too far away so that all the members of the family can participate. Keep the pace leisurely in order to enjoy the scenery as you bike along. Stop for rest as necessary. Take side trips if the kids think of something they want to see.

Variation: Plan a trip of a more challenging distance with a neighbor family. Make your destination a park or other pleasant spot where you can set up a portable grill. Designate someone to drive an R & R vehicle—a station wagon or van big enough to pick up those who need a rest (also to carry the grill and food). At your destination grill bratwurst or other favorite picnic food and enjoy getting to know your neighbors better. Then bike (or ride) back.

Make your own slippery slide. Using rocks or other heavy objects, anchor a large piece of plastic, such as a painter's drop cloth, and let water from the hose run down the plastic. Taking turns, kids can get a running start and slide down the sheet for hours of fun.

Other things that can keep kids busy for hours:

- a pack of water balloons
- a pile of scrap lumber (hammer, nails, etc.)
- games (see below).

Nostalgia Games

Don't accept the myth that kids who have played computer games can't enjoy the simple games their parents and grandparents played as kids, such as jacks, hide-and-seek, hopscotch, and jumping rope. Sift through your memory for some of your favorites and teach them to your kids. (And encourage your kids to ask their grandparents about the games they used to play.) Here are just a few from our family memory banks:

Red light, green light. One person is the traffic cop (officer, if you prefer) and all the other kids string out in a line at the other end of the yard, facing him or her. When the traffic cop yells, "Green light," everyone may run ahead. When the traffic cop yells, "Red light," everyone must stop. Anyone who doesn't stop immediately has to go back and start over while the others continue ahead. The traffic cop will want to give commands in quick succession to make the other players go when they should stop and stop when they should go. Whoever reaches the traffic cop first wins.

Kick the can. Play this like hide-and-seek, but add another fun feature to it. Set up a tin can at home base on a sidewalk or driveway. When a person gets back to home base without being caught, he "kicks the can," and the noise, which can generally be heard throughout the neighborhood, alerts the other players that someone has won. They can all return to begin again. (For

some reason this game seems most fun when played at dusk.)
House ball. A palm-sized rubber ball (or tennis ball) and the side of a house or garage (preferably without a window) is all that is needed. Kids take turns throwing the ball against the house and trying to clap before they catch it. The first time they throw it, they have to clap once. The second time, they have to clap twice, and so on. If the first person misses, it's the other person's turn, and the first person has to begin at the beginning on his or her next turn. Make the goal ten claps or whatever is agreed upon. (This can also be played alone.)

All About the Town

Parents can't be on the go all the time, but when the kids want to do something special once in a while, here are a few suggestions:

Become a home-town tourist. Write to your state's tourism department or local chamber of commerce for brochures about places to go and things to see. Make your plans and enjoy.

Museums—any kind can be interesting to kids—historical museums, science museums, art museums. Many of these places are becoming more sensitive to their younger patrons, designing their displays to pique the interest of kids. Make inquiries with your librarian or city or county officials to find out what is available in your area.

Often different aspects of a particular museum will appeal to different kids. One mom took her kids to the home of the first governor of their state. Her daughter was fascinated by the display of wedding dresses from various periods, while her son was more interested in Indian artifacts and the construction of the building. (A cut-away portion of the wall encased in glass showed the unique way the house was built, far different than today's methods.)

If you live within a few hours of a major city, take an occasional one-day trip to visit their planetarium, botanical gardens, science museums, or historical societies.

There are also many "living-history" sites around the country now, too, where people dress in costume from a particular period of history and assume identities of real or made-up characters from that time, acting, talking, working, and playing as people would in that era. This is a wonderful way of giving kids a realistic sense of history.

Lunch with Dad at work. Surprise Dad at work with a picnic lunch to be eaten on the grounds of his place of employment. (When a surprise lunch isn't appropriate, make arrangements ahead of time.) If possible, have Dad give the kids a tour of the building and show them what he does there.

If Mom works outside the home and circumstances permit, Dad may want to take some time off to arrange a family picnic where she works.

A meal or a day with Grandma and Grandpa. One child alone with grandparents for a meal can be a special experience. Sitting across the table from grandparents, face-to-face, and talking about anything the child wishes can make that child feel important and grown up. If grandparents can give the child a whole or a half day to play games or go someplace unusual, that's a treat, too.

Time with other relatives. Older grade-schoolers can be a great help to a cousin or aunt with a new baby, or they can do some cleaning for an aunt and uncle worn out with preschoolers. Somehow cleaning at someone else's house is a lot more fun than helping Mom clean at home.

Some of Joyce's fondest childhood memories are of the times she spent a whole week at an aunt's house, helping with major cleaning jobs and the care of younger cousins while her uncle was out of town.

Tours of businesses, shops, factories, etc. Moms report success in taking family tours of such places as pickle factories, newspaper print shops, power or water plants, airports, and train stations.

Activity Guidelines

Many times moms feel like the Lone Ranger, having total responsibility for their kids' happily-ever-after times at home. But even the Lone Ranger had Tonto. We can often take advantage of *some* of the church and community offerings, such as Vacation Bible Schools, camps, library story times, community classes, playground time, craft classes, and summer school.

Those mothers who prefer spontaneity or are prone to overscheduling themselves and their kids may want to find the programs that don't require a regular commitment.

Neighbors and friends from church, whether they have children or not, can also be good resources. One woman remembers her father "talking straight" to neighbor kids about marijuana and teaching them how to play sports. Retired people often enjoy being around young people, too. They can captivate kids with stories and encourage new skills.

Finding the Comfort Zone

How many activities we schedule depends on our kids' energy level (and ours) as well as their goals (and ours). Mothers who tend to overschedule themselves may also tend to overschedule their kids. Life is a series of choices, and sometimes the choices are tough. There are so many good activities from which to choose. None of us can do it all. As we parents make tough choices, we can also help our kids learn to manage their personal resources just as we want them to learn to manage financial resources. These are both survival skills.

Once parents and children alike have found the activity level with which they are comfortable (moms need to be honest about how much chauffeuring they can handle), it will be easier to relax and enjoy the times when the kids are home. Sometimes families will do things together. Other times family members may do things separately. Above all, we will want to honor God in our fun as well as our more serious moments.

——————— *Looking Up* ———————

Lord of joy,
> *Help us*
> *not to think*
> *that abundant life*
> *means abundant activity.*
> *Guide our choices*
> *and help our children*
> *give their best—*
> *not for us,*
> *but to You.*

Amen.

◇ **12** ◇

Remember When . . .

As the family is sitting around the dinner table with a guest, the conversation turns to the subject of people who have southern accents. One of the kids says, "Remember what Patty was like by the time we came home from our vacation in Tennessee? (The name has been changed to protect the embarrassable.) Everyone laughs except the dinner guest, who looks puzzled, left out.

It's a family joke. Patty hadn't been in Tennessee more than twenty-four hours before she had a drawl that would put a native Tennesseean to shame. But until the whole story was explained to the guest, that little remember-sentence meant nothing.

The conversation continues, and the kids reminisce about the people they met, their dinner at the Chattanooga Choo-Choo restaurant, and visits to Civil War battlefields.

It may be a cliché, but memories *are* precious.

Creating Memories?

Much has been written about making, building, or creating memories for our kids, but can we really *make* memories? At times, trying to create memories seems like trying to create sunshine. Memories happen. We can't always produce them. We can try to create the atmosphere in which a pleasant experience can become a memory, but often the things we so carefully plan are forgotten, and little things that happened spontaneously stick in our kids' minds (and ours) forever.

Joyce's son often teases her about his all-too-vivid memory of the time she closed his face in the car trunk. After loading luggage and other belongings into the trunk on a family trip, she slammed the lid, not realizing that he had leaned in to grab something to play with in the car. Fortunately, he received only a few minor cuts and scratches. She certainly hadn't *planned* that memory, yet he will never forget it, nor will he ever let *her* forget it.

Some books on memory making look like activity books, giving the impression that if we keep our kids busy all the time with parent-planned handcrafts and projects, that is the key to happy memories. But when asked about memories of their grade-school years, Joyce's kids didn't mention any handcrafts or projects they had done. They talked mostly about common things, such as snow forts, climbing trees, roller skating in their large rec room, biking along the creek path, seeing the family cat's kittens moments after they were born and watching them grow, and going to a local pizza place that had a window through which the kids could watch the cooks making pizzas.

Other memories, perhaps not so common, included spur-of-the moment trips, like the Memorial Day that they started out from their home in Minneapolis for a drive with no particular destination in mind. They ended up in St. Cloud, a smaller city about seventy miles away, and spent the day exploring the town. In the evening, when they saw the freeway's bumper-to-bumper traffic headed back into the Twin Cities, they decided to stay overnight—no previous reservations, no luggage, no change of clothes, no preparations whatsoever. The kids loved it.

Spontaneity and unpredictability are often the keys to fun memories.

Needing a chance to get away, one couple asked their kids to go play outside, and the parents secretly packed suitcases for everyone. Then they told the kids to get in the car, and they traveled to a nearby city for a weekend of relaxation together around the motel pool.

Joyce's kids also remember the time they helped her kidnap their dad, blindfold and all, for a much-needed parental weekend getaway.

But parents don't have to create elaborate events or leave town to provide fun memories for their kids. Creating an atmosphere for memories can also mean just keeping life interesting at home. It helps to be a little crazy. Parental tickle fights, harmless practical jokes on family members, a little ice down an unsuspecting child's back—anything like that can produce fun memories for our children. One teenager said that if parents want to give their kids fun memories, they should try being nutty.

"Over seriousness" seems to be a common symptom of today's society. Harvard professor and child development authority Dr. T. Berry Brazelton talks about the memories of children born in the fifties, who say, "No one ever smiled when I was little."

Brazelton says, "I was horrified, and learned that they saw their parents as too serious, always wondering whether they were doing the right thing in their role as a parent."[1] Perhaps realizing that the children who were growing up in the fifties and sixties (who had no role models for fun) are today's parents, he continues, "I fear that the same memories may dog children of [today]. 'No one ever smiles at our house' is a common complaint now. Everyone is too busy. There is likely to be no leeway for humor, for fun for its own sake."[2]

Christians, especially, are often accused of being too serious, and sometimes the criticism is justified. Although we do have a serious responsibility to pass along God's message, that doesn't mean we can't ever have fun. The Book of Proverbs extols the virtues of a cheerful heart. And we should be glad! Our sins are forgiven, our future is secure in Christ, and we have God's presence in our lives to handle any crisis that may arise. Christians, above all people, should enjoy life.

Having fun can balance the discipline we build into our family lives. We need that balance. And memories don't *all* have to be silly.

One family has vivid memories of the summer they slaved together with pickaxes and shovels in 98-degree weather to level their backyard and build a swimming pool. Their reward was a refreshing swim on their town's first 100-degree day in 24 years.

Each family has its own personality and various types of memories, and each individual in a family will remember different incidents and various aspects of the same event.

The Value of Memories

Regardless of whether they are pleasant or unpleasant, memories are priceless. In their book *Building Happy Memories and Family Traditions*, authors Birkey and Turnquist say, "Everyone needs a storehouse of precious memories that enhance a sense of belonging, a sense of being loved, a sense of worth, a sense of competence."[3]

A sense of belonging. We probably all know the feeling of hearing relatives discuss an incident from our family's past that we should remember but don't. It's frustrating. We somehow feel that, at least for that moment, we don't belong.

Common memories bind a family together. Activities such as trips, family reunions, exploring Grandma's attic, playing games that are family favorites, reading together, and a family-only church service when we were snowed in give us a sense of identity.

A sense of being loved. A simple memory like the Van Klompenburgs' usual bedtime story, hug, and pulling the covers up over the child before turning off the light is a memory of their parents' love that the kids won't easily forget.

Birkey and Turnquist pass along a grown woman's memory of an incident that occurred during the depression. At great sacrifice, her father had given her a dime to go to the local swimming pool—a real treat. But she lost the dime on her way to the pool. Bitterly disappointed, she headed back home, crying, knowing she wouldn't be able to go swimming. Her father, a traveling salesman, happened to come by just then, and upon hearing her story, dried her tears and spoke kindly to her. Then he reached into his pocket and gave her another dime. She *knew* what that cost him. She knew she was loved.

When children have memories of their parents sacrificing

something of themselves for their kids' happiness, that love is a solace and comfort when the children are older and need someone to turn to.

A sense of worth. The memory of a simple compliment, of a parent's time spent alone with one child, or of the encouragement of the child's curiosity, can strengthen a child's sense of self-worth.

One woman has pleasant childhood memories of finding tadpoles in a stream near her house. When she told her mother, her mom gave her a Mason jar and told her to catch some so she could study them awhile. Incidents like this assure our children that we are interested in whatever is important to them.

A sense of competence. When our kids have a memory of having done something well, they will have more confidence in their abilities to try the same thing again or something new.

One woman who seeks to use her singing talent for the Lord feels she probably never would have pursued music had it not been for the encouragement of others. One of her first memories of affirmation came when she was very young and an uncle asked her to sing in his church.

Memories can help shape a child's total self-concept.

Teaching Kids to Make Their Own Memories

We do not always have to be part of our children's memories, however. Some of their memories have to be their own. But sharing *our* memories with our kids, in effect, shows them the types of things that are worth remembering and how they can make their own memories.

Carol's kids often ask for "old-days stories," tales of what life was like when she and her husband were kids. They love to hear catastrophe stories like the one about the flood, during which Carol sat on the basement steps holding her baby brother as the water swirled around below. Her mother was hunting for Carol's father, who was late getting the cows in from the pasture.

But Carol's kids also enjoy hearing stories about their mom's favorite doll, her stuffed horse who lost his mane, and the spectacular kite her family built that was so big they could hardly hold it down in the breeze.

When we don't control our kids too tightly, when we allow them to take risks and try some things on their own (appropriate to their maturity level), we give them the freedom to succeed and the freedom to fail, as well. And sometimes the memories of failures can steer our kids clear of similar mistakes in the future.

Preserving Memories

Just as memories differ from one family to another, so will their means of preserving them.

Scrapbooks. Carol puts together family scrapbooks, saving such memory triggers as pictures the kids entered in coloring contests, bowling scores, and notes to and from various family members. She knows that many of these gems would mean little to anyone else, but someday when the kids are gone, she knows those scrapbooks will be an enjoyable way to look back and relive many happy times with her kids. Memories aren't just for our children. They're for us, too.

Photos. For one of Carol's sons, photos became an important way to preserve memories—especially in the case of his beloved kitten, which was hit by a speeding car. The pictures he had taken earlier became a source of comfort to him, helping him through his grief, and providing happy memories that enabled him to move on.

Journals. Some mothers encourage their children to keep journals of their thoughts and the things they do, especially over the summer. The kids will enjoy these memories for years to come. One mother encourages her children to make a combination scrapbook and journal, writing down some of their thoughts and activities but also including photos, papers, greeting cards, or other items of sentimental value.

Memory boxes. Many families have boxes in which they store memorabilia, but self-described "reformed clutter shufflers" Alice Fulton and Pauline Hatch recommend having a special memento box for each member of the family. They say,

> A grocery-store cardboard orange or apple box with a lid

makes a good starter box . . . We suggest you eventually invest in a quality container—perhaps even one that's custom-made, with hinged lid. This should be as nice as the contents, an heirloom in itself.

Baby books, scrapbooks, photo albums, ancestral heirlooms, vacation mementos, a last doll or treasured toy, and baby booties are some contents suggestions. A large manila envelope (one for each child) could hold school report cards and selected school papers.[4]

For Christmas one year a mom whose children were starting to leave home one by one took Fulton and Hatch's suggestion and asked a professional woodworker to craft a beautifully finished cube-shaped oak memento box measuring about 18" square (big enough to hold a large photo album) for each of her kids. These certainly will be treasured heirlooms, especially as the kids have filled them with precious memorabilia from their lives.

If we want to preserve memories, we have to give ourselves (and our children) permission to save and permission to throw. Depending on our personality type, one of these two things is probably more difficult than the other. For confessed (or closet) pack rats, saving comes naturally. For highly efficient housekeepers, saving may be more difficult unless they can see a practical use for the item.

But saving, especially in a limited container such as a memory box, usually requires a continuing sorting process. We can't keep everything that may someday have worth or sentimental value. We may save something today which tomorrow won't seem that important. That's when we need to give ourselves permission to throw things away—even if they were very important to us at one time—to make way for new items.

The Difference Between Memories and Traditions

Memories and traditions are not necessarily the same thing, but sometimes an event that becomes a pleasant memory is repeated frequently and becomes a tradition.

A number of years ago, Joyce's sister Jeanne began a Halloween practice that the whole family enjoyed. It quickly became a tradition. Wanting to get to know the neighbors and to have a testimony in the neighborhood, Jeanne and her husband set up a table in their front yard to serve hot apple cider and coffee to the parents who escorted their young trick-or-treaters around the block. Along with the candy, attractive Halloween tracts (written especially for kids) went into the kids' bags. On the usually chilly Minnesota October evenings, the parents appreciated the hot drink and the opportunity to visit.

Every year the practice grew. Jeanne started serving doughnuts, a friend began bringing his popcorn cart, and the gathering soon became an open house for many neighbors, friends, and relatives.

Their kids loved this family tradition, which then became a *neighborhood* tradition. When their family moved several years later, the neighbors showed great disappointment, wondering who would fill the gap. Jeanne and her husband now carry on this Halloween tradition in their new neighborhood.

Traditions, as well as memories, are important. Many of today's parents were part of the 60s generation, for whom *tradition* was a bad word. But now many of these same people are seeing the importance of traditions or rituals that bind a family together.

Some have realized the value of tradition through their children. If the kids enjoy a certain activity, such as hot chocolate and cookies in front of the fireplace while they open gifts on Christmas Eve, they become comfortable with it, and they want to do it again and again.

A Christmas tradition that the Ellis kids have enjoyed is the unusual gift tags their parents make. Mom and Dad usually try to give several small gifts rather than buying something expensive. Instead of writing "from Mom and Dad" on each gift, Joyce and her husband began pretending the gifts came from people who were important in their kids' eyes (e.g. sports figures, biblical and historical characters, authors).

A gift for their son, an avid Vikings fan, might be marked "from Anthony Carter," his favorite wide receiver at the time. A present for one of their daughters might be "from Laura Ingalls Wilder" while the child was engrossed in that series of books. Another daughter, who has been studying American History, may find a gift "from Abraham Lincoln." Even a present for Dad might be marked "from Agatha Christie," one of *his* favorite authors.

A different kind of tradition began when another family saw the Christmas cards that came each year as opportunities to remember their friends in prayer. Each day during their family devotions of the Christmas season, they prayed for the people whose cards had come in the mail that day.

Still another family found a new extended-family tradition when Grandma decided to sponsor a Fourth-of-July family camp-out for her grandchildren each year. She bought an old tent at a garage sale, and she and her grandkids camp out in the family farm's pasture by a river. The highlight is Grandma's fireworks show in the evening. Then the next morning, the first grandchild to arise wakens Grandma, who lights firecrackers to wake the rest.

Traditions of Giving

To avoid becoming too self-centered as a family, especially at Christmastime, some families have instituted traditions of giving to others in some way. "I view it as a way to give a gift to Christ," one mom said. "After all, it is His birthday we are celebrating." Jesus said, "Whatever you did for one of the least of these brothers of mine, you did for me" (Matthew 25:40). Some families look for a different project each year; others do the same thing from year to year.

One Christmas, a family with three kids "adopted" a Hmong family their church was sponsoring and let their kids buy gifts for the three Hmong children. Mom and Dad selected gifts for the parents as well. They worked together to wrap the presents and delivered them on Christmas Eve. Because they took pictures as all the gifts were opened, they can remember the delight on the children's faces, especially. They have great memories of the joy of giving.

One year when Joyce was volunteering at a hospital, she realized that carolers didn't come to sing for the patients on Christmas Day—an especially lonely time for many patients. Since the Ellises opened their gifts on Christmas Eve and didn't gather with the extended family until Christmas afternoon, they decided that they could spend an hour or two caroling as a family in the morning. Some years they invited other families and singles who were also free at that time.

As they strolled the corridors singing the joy of Christ's coming to earth, often the nurses, doctors, aides, and maintenance people would stop for moments and just listen, or they would urge them to come to their stations. People in the coronary-and-cancer care areas seemed especially eager for them to come their way. The Ellises soon realized that those who had to work on Christmas may have appreciated the music as much or more than the patients. And the family enjoyed an opportunity to give to others.

A further joy came when they discovered that one family they had invited to go with them began a similar tradition with a few families in their new church when they moved to another city.

Although the above examples all center around Christmas, we can establish traditions of giving any time of the year— helping at a food shelf, adopting a nursing-home resident to visit regularly, or even volunteering to work together as a family to clean the church building.

The Problem With Comparisons

Many families have all kinds of traditions and rituals for Christmas, Thanksgiving, Easter, birthdays, bedtime, preparing for a new year of school, service to others, almost every aspect of their family life. We could list more traditions shared by the mothers we surveyed, but for many people, reading through a list of other people's traditions doesn't help that much. Because of the difference in family personalities, what is meaningful for one family might sound rather silly to another.

Family rituals grow out of the family personality. Sometimes other people's practices can spark ideas for our own family, but many rituals are more meaningful if they are traditions we have invented, knowing ourselves and our kids. Having been fashioned in the image of our Creator, we all can be creative in one way or another. But we can't afford to compare ourselves to other families. God didn't create us all alike.

Preserving Traditions

When you find your own unique traditions, hold on to them. Rituals are healthy for a family. In fact, that was one of Dolores Curran's fifteen traits mentioned in Chapter 1: "The healthy family has a strong sense of family in which rituals and traditions abound."[5]

Regarding the importance of traditions, Christian sociologist and media personality Tony Campolo says,

> Those families that have a great deal of ritual are usually the ones that are the most solid and secure. They seem better able to impart to their children the values and truths which they believe to be of ultimate significance. . . . Rituals are good for families, and instituting rituals makes family life more fun for everyone.[6]

Some families will have more traditions than others. That's okay. This isn't a contest. But we can all find some rituals that bind us together. And just as memories can lead to traditions, traditions can give our kids (and their parents) many good memories.

Campolo also admits a very personal reason for insisting on certain rituals, especially at Christmas. He says,

> In the afternoons, we always visited my mother and then my in-laws. Visiting our children's grandparents was deliberately made into a ritual because I know that someday I will be a grandparent and I will eagerly await visits from my children's families. I feel sure that they will come to visit me because visiting parents on Christmas Day has become part of our family ritual.[7]

But rituals are one of those things that we hold on to with an open hand, knowing that when our kids have children of their own, they won't be able to follow *all* of our traditions. They will begin some of their own, often a combination of our traditions and those of the family into which they marry.

Launching Our Kids

In some ways that mixed response we feel when we load our children onto the school bus at the end of summer each year prepares us just a bit for that day when we unload our kids' belongings in their college dorm room or help them pack to move into their own apartment. There's a tear in our eye (however we may try to hide it) at the same time something inside us is cheering that our kids are entering a new, more grown-up phase of their lives.

Bruno Bettelheim, one of the foremost child psychologists in the world today, says, "Since the future is always uncertain, we cannot know what particular problems our child will encounter in life; therefore the best we can give him on his way into life is our trust in him and a sense of his own great worth."[8]

Christian parents could also add to that the gift of a healthy and "tried" trust in God.

Our children are traveling a rough road from dependence to independence. Sometimes there are curves and potholes, but we keep moving forward—in our own parenting style—and gradually turn over the keys to them.

Quit worrying about the experts, and start listening to your heart. Be realistic in your expectations, accept the rough times as growing experiences, and enjoy the special opportunities that only come *When the Kids Are Home From School*.

_____ *Looking Up* _____

Eternal Lord,
>*deliver us*
>*from being too serious;*
>*help us make life fun*
>*and memorable.*
>*Lord of the past,*
>*Lord of the future,*
>*we yield*
>*our kids*
>*to Your constant care.*

Amen.

"Now may the Lord of peace himself give you peace at all times and in every way. The Lord be with all of you" (2 Thessalonians 3:16).

10 Things Dad Can Do to Make Life Easier for a Summer Mom

In the summer most moms see Dad's coming home as an oasis in their day, in the same way that he looks forward to coming home for a break. While most dads will help out with the care of their children, sometimes they need a little prompting, a few reminders that moms can't do it alone. Spouses would do well to discuss this situation together when they are fresh and relaxed, and together come up with ideas that would be particularly helpful in their family situations. Here are some starter suggestions for dads, contributed by both men and women:

1. Remember when you come home from work that Mom is tired, too, having the responsibility for the kids all day. Whether or not she works outside the home, she has probably faced as much stress as you have. Ask if there's anything you could do to help with dinner, or just play with the kids outside for a while.

2. Take responsibility for your kids as much as possible when you're home.

3. When your wife mentions an errand or project that she would appreciate being done as soon as possible, try to comply. If you can't get to it immediately, write yourself a note so you won't forget about it. Don't be like Pa Kettle, who when seeing a job that needed to be done, sat in his rocking chair and

drawled, "I'm gonna have to fix that one of these days."

4. Even if you aren't a cook, the family would love something done on the grill. This is an excellent way to give Mom a break.

5. Don't be afraid of traditional "women's work." Dads are just as capable of mopping a floor or scrubbing a toilet; and incidentally, those chores are not that pleasant to women either.

6. Read aloud to the kids in the evening. They'll love it, and it's better than television.

7. Take the kids out for an occasional fast-food meal so that your wife can have a little time for herself. (Bring home some food for her, too.)

8. Play board games in the evening with your kids. Invite Mom to play, too, or give her an opportunity to sneak in a nap or a responsibility-free shopping trip.

9. Pack up the kids and take them to the park, a Little League game, or some other community event.

10. Rally the kids to help set the table for dinner and/or help in the meal preparation. Encourage *their* thoughtfulness by pointing out that Moms need a break sometimes, too.

Add your own ideas!

◊ Appendix A ◊

Summer-Moms Questionnaire

S ome of the fifty mothers who answered our summer survey told us that writing the answers to our questions each week helped them. Thinking through their answers gave them an appreciation for their families, a better understanding of their family dynamics, and a sense of distance from which to see the summer's events. Some saved copies of their answers for a summer journal.

In case you would like to answer some of the same questions they did, we've listed them below. Like the moms in our survey, you are free to skip any question to which you have no response.

Planning Ahead

(Not all mothers have plan-ahead summers, but if you do, you may wish to answer these questions.)

1. What preparations or planning ahead have you done for summer? _____
   _____
   _____
   _____

2. Please describe any daily routine you have in mind for your family. _____
   _____

_____

3. What chores and duties will be assigned each of your children?

_____

_____

4. How will you keep your kids performing these duties? _____

_____

_____

5. How much television do you plan for your children to watch?

_____

6. What will be your system for regulating TV time? _____

_____

_____

7. What will you do to bridge the transition from school routine to summertime? _____

_____

_____

8. Do you have a plan for your family worship and devotional life?

_____

What is it? _____

_____

_____

_____

WEEK 1

1. Is your summer taking shape as you pictured it? _____
Explain. _____

_____

_____

2. What is your family's eating routine? _____

_____

3. How do you handle snacking between meals and requests for additional food an hour before mealtime? _____
_____

4. Record a favorite recipe for snack food. _____
_____
_____
_____

5. Record a favorite mealtime recipe. _____
_____
_____
_____

6. Describe a project or activity that your children enjoy. _____
_____
_____

7. Tell a story, any story, about an event in your family life this week. _____
_____
_____
_____
_____

WEEK 2

1. Our best activity this week was _____
_____

2. Our major difficulty at this point is _____
_____

3. We are coping with it by _____
_____

4. One helpful technique for coping with clutter and dirt is _____
_____
_____

5. One way of dealing with fights and quarrels that I find helpful
is _____
_____
_____

6. I am finding personal time by _____
_____
_____

7. My best story for this week is _____
_____
_____
_____
_____

WEEK 3

1. How do you encourage reading or academic work in the summer? _____
_____
_____

2. How do you deal with visits from neighborhood children? _____
_____
_____

3. What do you do for inexpensive family outings? _____
_____
_____

4. What money-making projects have your children found? _____
_____
_____

5. Do you have time-alone-with-mom activities for your kids? _____
Describe them. _____
_____
_____
_____

6. How is Dad involved in the family summer? _____

_____

_____

WEEK 4

1. What do you do with your devotional time? _____

_____

Your personal time? _____

_____

2. Name one time-saving hint you would like to share. _____

_____

3. A family high point this week was _____

_____

4. A family low point this week was _____

_____

5. If I could wave a magic wand and change one family pattern for the rest of the summer I would _____

_____

_____

6. Tell a story from this week. _____

_____

_____

_____

WEEK 5

1. Does mothering ever seem similar to a roller coaster ride? ___ Explain. _____

_____

_____

2. Describe several indoor, at-home activities your children are enjoying this summer. _____

_____

_____

_____

_____

_____

3. What do you do when your kids say they are bored? _____

_____

_____

4. Our most dramatic moment this week was _____

_____

_____

5. When I run out of energy, I _____

_____

_____

WEEK 6

1. What recipe do your kids enjoy using? _____

_____

2. To help my children remember to close the door, I _____

_____

3. To teach my children to put away what they use, I _____

_____

4. When my children nag and whine, I _____

_____

_____

5. What is the best hour of your day? _____
The worst? _____

6. Write one brief story, recording an event of this week. _____

_____

_____

_____

WEEK 7

1. Describe an outdoor, at-home activity your children enjoy. ___

___

___

2. How does your physical and emotional condition now compare to what it was the first week of vacation? _____

___

3. How does your children's physical and emotional condition now compare to that of the first week of vacation? _____

___

___

4. This summer, I think God is teaching me _____

___

5. I wish God would also teach me _____

___

6. What special measures do you take for the times the kids are home alone? _____

___

___

___

7. Write a story, recording one event from this week. _____

___

___

___

WEEK 8

NO QUESTIONS. TAKE A VACATION!

WEEK 9

1. When I think of school starting in a month, I feel _____

___

___

2. As a summertime mom, I am least secure with _____

___

_____

_____

3. My favorite parenting book is _____

4. My kids' favorite books at the moment are _____

_____

5. A high point this week was _____

_____

6. A low point this week was _____

_____

WEEK 10
The questions moms asked us to ask you

1. How do you regulate children's use of the telephone? _____

_____

2. How many nights a week do you allow your children to be away at a friend's house overnight? _____

_____

3. How do you encourage children to take more pride in their belongings, to take better care of their clothes, books, rooms, etc.? _____

_____

_____

_____

4. How do you remain consistent? _____

_____

5. Do you ever feel guilty about not having friends over for coffee more often? _____
   What do you do about it? _____

_____

6. How do you recharge and prepare for a new day? _____

_____

_____

WEEK 11

1. Some ways my children filled their time during car travel this summer were _____

_____

_____

_____

2. Some junk my kids used creatively this summer was _____

_____

_____

3. My kids' favorite memory from this summer will probably be

_____

_____

_____

4. My expectations for this summer were _____

_____

_____

5. Compared to my expectations, this summer was _____

_____

_____

6. If you used charts this summer, describe your success or failure with them. _____

_____

_____

_____

WEEK 12

One final question:

As soon as your children get on the bus to begin school again, sit down at a table or typewriter and begin writing, starting with these words:

> Summer is over. It's the first day of school. The kids have left, and I'm thinking . . . I'm feeling . . .

Let the words flow. Don't worry about proper grammar, handwriting, or even about staying on the subject. Simply write whatever pops into your head. Write as much or as little as you want to.

If your mind goes blank for a moment, write again, "It's the first day of school and I'm thinking . . ." See what thoughts pop into your mind. You may be surprised by what you discover about your thoughts and feelings.

◇ Appendix B ◇

Chores Grade-school Kids Can Do

You may want to arrange these chores into age-appropriate categories. Every child differs in his/her maturity level, personality, and physical capability.

Personal Hygiene:
- ☐ wash face
- ☐ comb hair
- ☐ brush teeth
- ☐ shower/bathe
- ☐ shampoo

Own Bedroom Care:
- ☐ make bed
- ☐ straighten and organize
- ☐ dust
- ☐ vacuum

Bathroom Cleaning:
- ☐ straighten
- ☐ clean sinks, tub, shower stall
- ☐ clean mirrors
- ☐ clean toilet (many moms prefer to take responsibility for this)

Cleaning Other Rooms:
- ☐ straighten

☐ dust
☐ sweep, vacuum, mop

Laundry:
☐ collect and/or sort
☐ hang on line or put in dryer
☐ remove from line or dryer
☐ iron
☐ fold
☐ put away in drawers

Vehicle Care:
☐ wash exterior
☐ vacuum interior
☐ clean dash, windows, door panels, vinyl upholstery

Yard Work:
☐ water yard, garden, flowers
☐ weed garden
☐ mow, rake
☐ sweep sidewalk, patio
☐ harvest garden
☐ scrape and paint outdoor fence or deck
☐ help preserve garden produce

Mealtime Help:
☐ help plan menus
☐ help select groceries for planned menus
☐ set table
☐ make (or help make) meal
☐ clear table
☐ load dishwasher (or wash and dry dishes)
☐ put away dishes

Snack Preparation:
☐ prepare or bake a snack
☐ clean-up

Other Chores:
☐ babysit for younger siblings
☐ collect trash from wastebaskets
☐ take out the trash
☐ sweep garage
☐ feed and care for family pets

- ☐ help make family scrapbook
- ☐ help fill family photo album
- ☐ write a letter to relatives
- ☐ collect mail
- ☐ clip, organize, and sort coupons
- ☐ clean windows
- ☐ clean a closet
- ☐ straighten dresser drawers
- ☐ organize toys and games

◇ Appendix C ◇

Easy and/or Cool-kitchen Recipes

Salads

PASTA SALAD
Recipe from the kitchen of: Ruth Bandstra, Massachusetts

1 lb. pasta spirals (cooked, drained, and cooled)
4 C. assorted fresh vegetables, diced (broccoli, red onion, peppers, artichokes, cauliflower, cucumber, radishes, etc.)
1 lg. bottle zesty Italian dressing
2 tsp. SPIKE (a seasoning)

Mix, chill, and serve. Serves 6–8.

COLD TUNA SALAD
Recipe from the kitchen of: Lynette Horwath, Wisconsin

2–3 C. veggie-type shell noodles, cooked and cooled
Salad dressing to moisten (equal parts mayonnaise and French, mixed)
1 can flaked tuna
1 chopped tomato
Chopped black olives
Chopped celery
Grated onion

Mix all ingredients. Chill for several hours before serving. Serves 4–6.

TACO SALAD MEAL
Recipe from the kitchen of: Beverly Smid, New Jersey

1 lb. ground beef
1 taco seasoning packet
1 large head of lettuce, torn into bite-size pieces
2 tomatoes, cut in chunks
Cheddar cheese

Brown ground beef and add taco seasoning according to packet directions. Mix lettuce, cheese, and tomatoes. Put beef atop salad and serve immediately. Serve with a bag of taco chips and salad dressing if desired. Round out the meal with hard rolls and butter and a large platter of sliced melon or other fruit. Serves 4–6.
Authors' note: You can also substitute picante sauce and/or sour cream in place of salad dressing.

CHINESE NOODLE SALAD
Recipe from the kitchen of: Joyce Ellis, Minnesota

2 cans tuna or chicken, drained and flaked
6 hard-boiled eggs, chopped
5–6 carrots, shredded
Mayonnaise or Miracle Whip to moisten
½ lb. seedless grapes or 1 20 oz. can pineapple chunks, drained
Crisp Chinese noodles

Mix all ingredients together except Chinese noodles. Add noodles just before serving. Serves 8–10.

MARINATED CARROTS
Recipe from the kitchen of: Carol Van Klompenburg, Iowa

2 lbs. carrots, sliced, cooked until crisp/tender
1 green pepper, sliced
1 onion, sliced
1 10½ oz. can condensed tomato soup
1 C. sugar
½ C. salad oil
¾ C. white vinegar
1 tsp. Worcestershire sauce

Drain carrots. Add green pepper and onion. Put other ingredients in blender. Blend well. Pour over vegetable mixture. Let stand overnight. Serve cold. Will keep well in the refrigerator for several days. Serves 6–8.

For an easier version, use canned carrots. It's not quite as tasty, but it is faster and saves heating up your kitchen.

REFRESHING SALAD (side dish)
Recipe from the kitchen of: Joyce Ellis, Minnesota

1 lg. or 2 sm. pkgs. lemon gelatin
2 C. boiling water
1 sm. can crushed pineapple, drained (reserve juice)
1 12-oz. can sugar-free grapefruit soda pop (or lemon-line, ginger ale, etc.)
1 9-oz tub Cool Whip
½ C. nuts, chopped
2–3 bananas, sliced

Dissolve gelatin in boiling water. Drain crushed pineapple. Add reserved juice and soda pop to dissolved gelatin. Chill until jiggly. Beat with wire whip. Fold in Cool Whip, pineapple, nuts, and bananas. Chill until set. Serves 6–8.

MACARONI SALAD
Recipe from the kitchen of: Kathy Viss, California

2 C. macaroni (cooked, drained, and rinsed)
1 C. diced celery
1 medium onion, diced
3 hard-cooked eggs, chopped
Cheddar cheese cubes (as much as you like)
2 C. frozen peas, defrosted

Dressing:
1 C. mayonnaise
¼ C. sugar
1 C. sweet pickle relish
2 tsp. mustard

Toss salad ingredients together in a large bowl. In separate bowl combine dressing ingredients. Pour over macaroni mixture and stir enough to coat all ingredients. Chill well before serving. Serves 4–6.

Optional ingredients: Add diced green peppers, cucumber, or whatever vegetables your family likes.

SEVEN-LAYER SALAD
Recipe from the kitchen of: Joyce Ellis, Minnesota

Put one layer of each of the following ingredients into a large bowl
in the order given:
1 whole head lettuce, torn into bite-size pieces
1 C. chopped celery
½ C. chopped green pepper
½ C. chopped onion (may use part green onion)
8 slices bacon, fried crisp and crumbled
1 C. frozen peas, cooked and drained
1 C. shredded cheddar cheese

Spread 1 pint mayonnaise on top. Seal with plastic wrap and let it
set overnight in the refrigerator. Serves 6–8.
Note: Add or delete ingredients according to your family's preferences. This salad is especially pretty in a large clear glass bowl.

Stove-top or Microwave Meals

OLD FAITHFUL IN A MICROWAVE
Recipe from the kitchen of: Carol Van Klompenburg, Iowa

1 lb. ground beef
1 small onion
4–5 medium potatoes, peeled and sliced
16 oz. frozen vegetables (peas, corn, or mixed veg.)
1 10½ oz. can cream of mushroom soup
1 10½ oz. can cream of chicken (or celery) soup

Break ground beef into small pieces in casserole dish. Slice in onion.
Microwave 4 minutes on high. Stir. Microwave an additional 2–4
minutes until meat is no longer pink.* Drain fat. Set aside. Slice
potatoes into a 2-qt. casserole. Cover and microwave 4 minutes on
high. Top with frozen vegetables and microwave an additional 8
minutes. Top with ground beef and onion mixture. Spread with
soups. Microwave on high for 15 minutes or until potatoes are
tender. Serves 4–6.

*If you prefer, you may brown the ground beef and onion in a
frying pan while the potatoes cook in the microwave.

SOUPER CHEESEBURGERS
Recipe from the kitchen of: Joyce Ellis, Minnesota

1 lb. ground beef or ground turkey
1 medium onion, chopped (or use dried minced onions)
1 can cheddar cheese soup
1 pkg. hamburger buns, split and toasted

Brown ground beef with onion and drain off fat. Stir in cheese soup until well blended. Keep over low heat until heated through. Serve on toasted hamburger buns like sloppy joes. Serves 4–6.

EASY-DO SPAGHETTI
Recipe from the kitchen of: Ginger Eskes, California

½ lb. lean ground chuck
½ C. chopped onion
1 clove garlic, minced
1 8-oz. can tomato sauce
1 C. whole, peeled tomatoes and juice, pureed
1 2-oz. can mushroom stems, pieces, and liquid
4 oz. uncooked spaghetti (1 C. of 2-inch pieces)
1 Tbsp. parsley flakes
¼ tsp. oregano, crushed
⅛ tsp. red hot pepper sauce
Dash cayenne pepper
1 C. shredded American cheese
¼ C. parmesan cheese
Chopped fresh parsley, optional

Combine beef, onion, and garlic in 2½ qt. casserole. Microwave on high for 3 minutes, stirring after 2 minutes. Add remaining ingredients except cheese, mixing well. Cover. Microwave on high for 14–16 minutes, stirring every 3 minutes. Sprinkle cheeses over top. Cover and let stand 5–10 minutes or until cheese is melted. Serves 4.

SLOPPY PIZZAS
Recipe from the kitchen of: Jeanne Williams, Minnesota

1 lb. ground beef
2 cloves garlic, finely minced
1 med. onion, chopped
¼ C. pimiento-stuffed olives, chopped
1 tsp. salt
½ tsp. sugar
½ tsp. pepper
1½ tsp. oregano
1 8-oz. can tomato sauce
1 6-oz. can tomato paste
4 oz. shredded mozzarella cheese, divided
Hamburger buns, split and toasted

Brown meat with garlic and onion. Drain. Add olives, salt, sugar, pepper, oregano. Then stir in tomato sauce and paste. Cook over low heat 30 minutes, stirring occasionally. Add half of the mozzarella just before serving. Serve on toasted bun halves, topped with remaining mozzarella. Serves 6.

BAKED POTATO MEAL
Recipe from the kitchen of: Joan Bear, Kentucky

Bake potatoes in the microwave to avoid heating up the kitchen. When fully baked, slice down the middle and chop up the insides a little. Serve with a variety of toppings: cooked broccoli, cheese, green onions, or canned chili heated in the microwave. Allow one potato per person or half a potato for the kids.

Complete the meal with tossed salad and sliced fruit.

HAWAIIAN HAYSTACK
Recipe from the kitchen of: Judy Oppewall, Iowa

2 cans cream of chicken soup
1 C. chicken broth or bouillon
2 C. cooked chicken (or turkey or gr. beef)
1 9-oz. pkg. chow mein noodles
2 med. tomatoes, diced
1 C. chopped celery
4 C. cooked rice
½ C. chopped green pepper
½ C. chopped onion
1 20-oz. can pineapple chunks, drained
1 C. grated cheddar cheese
½ C. chopped almonds
½ C. coconut
1 2-oz. jar pimiento

Combine soup and chicken broth. Blend well. Add meat. Simmer 8–10 minutes or microwave until heated through. Put remaining ingredients in individual serving bowls or in sections of a lazy susan. Each person can stack on their plate the rice, noodles, meat/gravy, and then toppings of their choice. Serves 6–8.
Note: Add mushrooms, sprouts or other family favorites to the above list and delete items your family does not like. This is a fun meal with guests.

BURRITOS
Recipe from the kitchen of: Dorothy Ter Horst, South Dakota

1 lb. ground beef
1 pkg. taco seasoning
1 can refried beans
Soft-shell tacos
Optional: cheese, green onion, lettuce, tomatoes, sour cream, hot
    sauce

Brown the ground beef and stir in the taco seasoning and refried beans. When hot, serve on soft-shell tacos. Let family members add other toppings according to their personal preferences. Serves 4–6.

MICROWAVE BURRITOS
Recipe from the kitchen of: Joyce Ellis, Minnesota

1 lb. ground beef or ground turkey
Dried minced onion to taste
Salt and pepper
Flour tortillas
1 can refried beans
8 oz. shredded cheddar cheese
Pace Picante Sauce (salsa)

Using stove top or microwave, brown meat and onions in skillet, adding seasonings to taste. Drain. Spread thin layer of refried beans in center of each tortilla. Add 2–3 tablespoons of meat. Sprinkle with cheese and top with picante sauce. Fold bottom third of tortilla up, bring ends in, and finish rolling up burrito style. Place seam-side down on microwave-safe plate and zap for about one minute at high heat in microwave or until heated through and cheese has melted. Serves 4–6.
Variation: For those who don't like Mexican food, omit refried beans and picante sauce, adding barbecue sauce instead.
Note: Keep all the ingredients in the refrigerator (including browned hamburger) so that the kids can help themselves for lunch.

MICROWAVE MEATBALLS
Recipe from the kitchen of: Carol Van Klompenburg, Iowa

1 10½ oz. can cream of mushroom soup
½ C. water
1 lb. ground beef
½ C. dry bread crumbs
1 Tbsp. parsley (or dill weed)
1 Tbsp. onion
1 egg, beaten

Mix soup and water. Set aside. Put remaining ingredients in separate bowl. Add ½ C. soup and water mixture. Mix well and shape into 1½-inch balls. Microwave on high 5 minutes. Rearrange meatballs for even cooking and microwave 4 more minutes or until done. Drain grease. Pour remaining soup mixture over meatballs and microwave 2 minutes or until soup mixture is hot. Serves 4–6.

CROCKPOT BAKED BEANS
Recipe from the kitchen of: Karen Wolthuis, Michigan

2 lg. jars northern beans
1½ C. white sugar
1 C. brown sugar
1 lg. onion, chopped
1 C. catsup
2 Tbsp. vinegar
2 tsp. dry mustard
16 slices bacon, cut in 1-inch pieces
2 cans French-fried onion rings

Mix all ingredients except onion rings. Cook in crockpot on high for 5–6 hours or on low for 10–12 hours. If it is not thick enough, remove the lid one hour before serving. Top with onion rings before serving. Both sugars can be reduced by ¼ C. Serves 6–8.

Recipes for *Cooler* Days (Oven Required)

POUR PIZZA
Recipe from the kitchen of: Robin Haack, Iowa

1 lb. ground beef
1 onion, chopped
1 C. flour
1 tsp. salt
⅛ tsp. pepper
⅛ tsp. oregano
2 eggs
⅔ C. milk
Small amt. cornmeal
1 15-oz. can pizza sauce
2 C. grated mozzarella cheese

Lightly brown hamburger and onion. Season with salt and pepper to taste. Set aside. Combine flour, salt, pepper, oregano, eggs, and milk, making a soft batter. Grease a 9 × 13 pan and sprinkle lightly with cornmeal. Pour batter into pan. Sprinkle meat over batter and bake at 400° for 15–20 minutes. Remove from oven. Spread pizza sauce on top and sprinkle with cheese. Return to oven and bake an additional 15 minutes. Serves 4–6.

BAKED CHICKEN WINGS
Recipe from the kitchen of: Jan Freeland, New Mexico

1 pkg. chicken wings (or other cut of chicken)
Lemon-pepper seasoning

Rinse chicken. Line a baking dish with aluminum foil (for less clean-up) or grease the baking dish. Place chicken in dish and season with lemon pepper. Bake at 400°. After 25 minutes, turn chicken and season other side. Cook for 20–25 minutes more. Serve with tossed rice, vegetable salad, bread, and a beverage.

HOT DOG BUNDLES
Recipe from the kitchen of: Kathy Viss, California

1 roll of ten refrigerator biscuits
1 pkg. of ten hot dogs (room temperature)

Slightly flatten each biscuit and wrap around the hot dog to make a bundle, pinching the edges tightly together to seal. Place sealed-edge down on greased baking sheet (can use non-stick spray). Bake according to instructions on the biscuit package until lightly browned and not doughy inside. Serve with catsup and mustard. Variation: When baked, place a slice of cheddar or American cheese atop the bundles. Return them briefly to oven to melt cheese.

Beverages

FRUIT SLUSH
Recipe from the kitchen of: Tammy Johnson, Minnesota

6 C. water
2 C. sugar
1 24-oz. can frozen orange juice, undiluted
6 large bananas
1 46-oz. can unsweetened pineapple juice

Bring water and sugar to boil and cool. Mix remaining ingredients in blender. Combine all ingredients in a 5-qt. ice cream pail. Freeze. To serve, scrape enough of the frozen mixture to half fill a glass. Fill remainder of glass with ginger ale. Stir and serve.

STRAWBERRY SLUSH
Recipe from the kitchen of: Esther Stoel, Indiana

3 C. skim milk
Sugar or artificial sweetener to taste
½ C. frozen strawberries
1 tsp. strawberry flavoring

Whirl in blender and "slurp it up." This may also be made with banana pieces, or frozen blueberries, omitting the strawberry flavoring. It's refreshing, nutritious, filling—and low-calorie.

SLUSH/POPSICLES
Recipe from the kitchen of: Joan Bear, Kentucky

Frozen juice concentrate
Carbonated water
Frozen fruit

Mix concentrate with the carbonated water according to concentrate directions. Add some frozen fruit, such as strawberries, and whirl in the blender. It makes a great drink, or you can freeze it for popsicles.

ICE CREAM SHAKE
Recipe from the kitchen of: Judy Oppewall, Iowa

2 scoops ice cream
¼ C. milk
2–3 C. fresh fruit (strawberries, bananas, etc.)

Whirl ingredients in blender for a few seconds; pour it into a glass. Put your feet up and cool off on a hot summer day.

PEACH JULIUS
Recipe from the kitchen of: Kathy Viss, California

5 heaping tsp. sugar, depending on sweetness of fruit
2 eggs
1 C. milk
¾ tsp. vanilla or almond flavoring
10 or more ice cubes
3–4 fresh peaches

Place all ingredients in a blender and process until the ice is finely chopped and the drink is frothy. You may substitute two cups orange juice for the peaches and have an orange julius.

HOME-BREWED ICED TEA
Recipe from the kitchen of: Joyce Ellis, Minnesota

6 tea bags
4 C. boiling water
1½ C. sugar
4 capsful of reconstituted lemon juice or the juice of one fresh lemon.

Pour boiling water over tea bags and let steep about fifteen minutes. Measure sugar into 1-gal. pitcher. Add lemon juice and a enough warm water to dissolve sugar. Remove tea bags, squeezing out extra liquid, and pour steeped tea mixture into pitcher. Stir. Add cold water to make one gallon. Serve over ice, and add a sprig of fresh mint leaves if desired.

Desserts

ELECTRIC FRYPAN UPSIDE-DOWN CAKE
Recipe from the kitchen of: Joyce Ellis, Minnesota

5 Tbsp. butter
1 C. brown sugar, firmly packed
1 #2 can (2½ C. pineapple slices or peach slices, drained
Maraschino cherries
Pecan halves
1 yellow cake mix
Whipped cream (optional)

Preheat frypan to 250°. Melt butter in pan, add brown sugar and mix well. Spread evenly on bottom of frypan. Arrange fruit and nuts over sugar mixture. Prepare cake mix according to directions. Spread evenly on top of fruit. Cover frypan, with vent open. Bake 30 minutes or until cake is dry on top. While cake is hot, loosen edges with a spatula. Place plate or tray over frypan and invert to remove cake. Lift off frypan. Serve warm or cold with whipped cream.

WACKY CAKE
Recipe from the kitchen of: Ona Vititoe, Missouri

1½ C. flour
1 C. sugar
¾ tsp. salt
1 tsp. baking soda
¼ C. cocoa
1 Tbsp. vinegar
⅓ C. salad oil
1 C. cold water
1 tsp. vanilla

Sift all ingredients into ungreased, 9 × 13 pan. Make three wells in dry ingredients. In one place vinegar, in second oil, and in third vanilla. Pour water over all and stir until mixed. No beating is needed. Bake at 350° for about 30 minutes or until top springs back when touched lightly.
Note: This isn't exactly a cool-kitchen recipe, but it's one that's easy and fun for kids to make. Try this on a cooler day.

PISTACHIO DESSERT
Recipe from the kitchen of: Joyce Ellis, Minnesota

1¼ C. graham cracker crumbs
¼ C. sugar
6 Tbsp. butter or margarine, melted
½ gal. vanilla ice cream (or ice milk or frozen yogurt)
1 sm. pkg. pistachio pudding mix
Green food coloring

Prepare graham cracker crust by combining first three ingredients in a small bowl. Reserve small amount of the mixture for topping. Press remaining crumb mixture into 8- or 9-inch square pan. Refrigerate. Place ice cream in large mixing bowl. Allow to soften to pudding consistency at room temperature, stirring occasionally. Add dry pistachio pudding mix and stir with wooden spoon until well blended. Fold in a few drops of food coloring for minty green color. Sprinkle reserved graham-cracker mixture on top. Freeze until firm. Serves 9–12.
Variation: Use crushed Oreo or Hydrox cookies in place of graham cracker crumbs.

NO-COOK MARSHMALLOW FROSTING
Recipe from the kitchen of: Joyce Ellis, Minnesota

2 egg whites
¼ tsp. salt
¼ C. sugar
¾ C. light corn syrup
1¼ tsp. vanilla

Beat egg whites and salt with electric beater until soft peaks form. Add sugar, about 1 tsp. at a time, beating until smooth and glossy. Continue beating and add corn syrup a little at a time, beating after each addition until frosting peaks. Fold in vanilla. Makes enough icing to fill and frost a 9" layer cake.

Snacks

WIGGLY FINGER WONDERFULS
Recipe from the kitchen of: Robin Haack, Iowa

3 pkgs. unflavored gelatin
¾ C. pineapple juice
1 C. boiling water
1 C. orange juice

Soften gelatin with a little pineapple juice. Add boiling water slowly, beating constantly until gelatin is dissolved. Add remaining juices. Pour into 9 × 13 pan. Chill until set. Cut into finger lengths. Variation: Substitute grape or cranberry juice for pineapple and orange juice.

MUD COOKIES
Recipe from the kitchen of: Carol Van Klompenburg, Iowa

½ C. milk
1 C. sugar
3 Tbsp. dry, unsweetened cocoa
⅓ C. margarine
½ C. chunky peanut butter
3 C. quick oats
1 tsp. vanilla

Combine milk, sugar, cocoa, and margarine in saucepan. Bring to a boil. Stir in peanut butter. Remove from heat. Quickly stir in oats and vanilla. Drop by tablespoonsful onto waxed paper. Let cool and serve.

ANTS ON A LOG
Recipe from the kitchen of: Joyce Ellis, Minnesota

Fill celery sticks with peanut butter and top with four to five raisins in a row.

Other celery fillings: peanut butter alone, pineapple or other flavored cream cheese, spreadable cheese—plain or various flavors.

PEAR POPSICLES
Recipe from the kitchen of: Faith Tibe, Iowa

Whirl a large can of pears, juice and all, in blender. Pour mixture into 3-oz. paper cups, insert popsicle sticks, and freeze. For fewer popsicles, use smaller can.
Note: Faith says, "My children may eat as many of these as they wish."

FROZEN PUDDING SANDWICHES
Recipe from the kitchen of: Betty Kimble, Iowa

1 pkg. instant pudding, banana or butterscotch
1¼ C. milk
2 C. Cool Whip
Graham crackers

Blend pudding with milk. Add Cool Whip and stir until blended. Spread a thick layer on a graham cracker. Top with a second graham cracker. Wrap individually in plastic wrap and freeze. Makes a cool, quick snack.

MICROWAVE CHIPS AND CHEESE
Recipe from the kitchen of: Joyce Ellis, Minnesota

Cover microwave-safe plate with taco chips, having chips overlapping slightly. Top with shredded cheese (cheddar, mozzarella, Monterrey jack, or any combination of the above). Microwave on high just until cheese is melted. Serve as is or with salsa.

MIX-UP SNACK
Recipe from the kitchen of: Kathy Vander Leest, Illinois

Cold cereal, any kind
Nuts
Raisins
Chocolate chips (or butterscotch chips or M & M's)
Miniature marshmallows

Mix any combination of these ingredients in a large bowl and then put into individual recloseable plastic bags for snacking. Kids love to mix these up—and eat them.

MICROWAVE S'MORES
Recipe from the kitchen of: Rachel Te Grootenhuis, Iowa

1 graham cracker (2 squares)
1 marshmallow
Chocolate chips

Place marshmallow atop half of the graham cracker. Microwave until it puffs up. Add chips. Microwave a few more seconds until the chips melt slightly. Press second half of cracker on top. Cool slightly and eat.

NO-BAKE PEANUT BUTTER COOKIES
Recipe from the kitchen of: Carol Van Klompenburg, Iowa

1 C. white sugar
1 C. white corn syrup
2 C. peanut butter
6 C. corn flakes

Bring sugar and syrup to a boil. Remove from heat. Add peanut butter. Stir. Add corn flakes and stir. Drop by tablespoonsful onto waxed paper. Cool and serve.

CAKE MIX COOKIES
Recipe from the kitchen of: Maureen Rank, Iowa

1 cake mix, any flavor
2 eggs
⅓ C. oil
1 tsp. vanilla

Mix together. Drop by teaspoonsful onto a greased cookie sheet.
Bake 8–10 min. at 325°.
The variations make it fun: To a chocolate chip mix we add
extra chips. To a chocolate mint mix, we add mint chips. Or for a
yellow cake mix, we make cookie balls and roll them in a sugar
and cinnamon mixture. We roll chocolate cake mix cookie balls in
powdered sugar, and add raisins to an oatmeal cake mix.
Note: Maureen says her six-year-old can do these alone except for
baking them. There's no messy flour, etc. to measure.

GRANOLA
Recipe from the kitchen of: Julane Lamkin, Michigan

3 C. old-fashioned oats
1 C. wheat germ
1 C. coconut, sweetened or unsweetened
2 tsp. ground cinnamon
2 Tbsp. brown sugar
¼ C. instant nonfat dry milk
½ C. honey
½ C. vegetable oil
1 tsp. vanilla
1 C. raisins
1 C. sunflower seeds
1 C. pitted, chopped dates

Heat oven to 250 or 300°. Mix first six ingredients in a large shallow
glass bowl. Combine honey, oil, and vanilla. Stir and heat until
blended. Drizzle over the dry ingredients. Bake for 1 hour at 250°
or 30 minutes at 300°, stirring several times. Cool and add raisins,
dates, and seeds. Serve for breakfast, snacks, or on ice cream. Can
also be used to make granola bars.

GRANOLA BARS
Recipe from the kitchen of: Julane Lamkin, Michigan

3 eggs, lightly beaten
3 C. granola (see granola recipe)
½ C. grated raw carrots

Preheat oven to 350°. Grease an 8″ square pan. Combine all ingredients and pat mixture evenly into the greased pan. Bake for 15 minutes. Cool slightly before cutting. Store in the refrigerator.

◇ Appendix D ◇

Recommended Children's Books

W hen looking for quality reading at your local library or book store, look for Newbery Award winners (best-written book of the year) and Caldecott Medal winners (best illustrated book of the year). In Christian publishing the Gold Medallion Award designates the best books of the year. There are many other good books available in both Christian and secular book stores—everything from social realism to fantasy. There is no way to list them all, but here are a few recommendations with notations of author, title, and publisher.

For Children in Early Grades

Carle, Eric. *The Very Hungry Caterpillar.* Philomel.

Carlson, Bernice Wells and Ristiina Wigg. *We Want Sunshine in Our Houses.* David K. Stone, illus., Abingdon.

Castle, Caroline. *The Hare and the Tortoise.* Peter Weevers, illus., Dial/Dutton.

De Paola, Tomie (storyteller and illustrator). *The Legend of Old Befana.* Harcourt Brace Jovanovich.

Field, Eugene. *Wynken, Blynken and Nod.* Barbara Cooney, illus., Hastings House.

Howe, James. *I Wish I Were a Butterfly.* Ed Young, illus., Harcourt Brace Jovanovich.

Jonas, Ann. *The Trek*. Greenwillow.

Marxhausen, Joanne. *3 in 1 (A Picture of God)*. Benjamin Marxhausen, illus., Concordia.

McKissack, Patricia C. *Lights Out Christopher*. Bartholomew, illus., Augsburg.

Parish, Peggy. *Amelia Bedelia*. Lynn Sweat, illus., Avon/Camelot. (also other titles by this author)

Taylor, Mildred D. *The Friendship*. Max Ginsburg, illus., Dial Press.

Wangerin, Walter Jr. *Thistle*. Marcia Sewell, illus., Harper & Row.

Williams, Barbara. *Kevin's Grandma*. Kay Chorao, illus., Scholastic Book Services.

Yolen, Jane. *Owl Moon*. John Schoenherr, illus., Philomel.

For Older Readers or Family Reading

Babbitt, Natalie. *Tuck Everlasting*. Farrar Straus Giroux.

Bond, Michael. *A Bear Called Paddington*. Dell.

Brink, Carol Ryrie. *Caddie Woodlawn*. Collier.

Brouwer, Sigmund. *The Disappearing Jewel of Madagascar*. Victor Books. (also other titles in The Accidental Detectives series)

Cleary, Beverly. *Ramona the Pest*. Scholastic Book Services. (also other titles by this author)

Dahl, Roald. *Charlie and the Chocolate Factory*. Bantam.

Fleming, Ian. *Chitty Chitty Bang Bang*. Scholastic Book Services.

Henry, Marguerite. *Misty of Chincoteague*. Rand McNally.

Jenkins, Jerry B. *The Clubhouse Mystery*. Moody. (also other titles in the Bradford Family Adventure series)

Johnson, Lois Walfrid. *The Disappearing Stranger*. Bethany House. (also other titles in her Adventures of the Northwoods series)

Konigsburg, E. L. *From the Mixed-up Files of Mrs. Basic E. Frankweiler*. Atheneum.

Lawhead, Stephen. *The Tale of Jeremy Vole*. Lion Pub.

Lawson, Robert. *Mr. Revere and I*. Dell. (also other biographies by this author)

Lenski, Lois. *Strawberry Girl*. Dell.

Leppard, Lois Gladys. *Mandie and the Secret Tunnel*. Bethany House. (also other titles in this series)

Lewis, C. S. *The Lion, the Witch, and the Wardrobe*. Collier. (also other titles in his Narnia series)

Lindgren, Astrid. *Pippi Longstocking*. Viking Press. (also other titles by this author)

MacDonald, Betty. *Hello, Mrs. Piggle Wiggle*. Lippincott. (Also other titles by this author)

MacDonald, George. *Wee Sir Gibbie of the Highlands*. Bethany House. (also other children's titles by this author)

MacGregor, Ellen. *Miss Pickerell Goes to Mars*. Scholastic Book Services. (also other titles by this author)

Milne, A. A. *Winnie the Pooh*. Dell. (also other titles by this author)

Robertson, Keith. *Henry Reed's Baby-sitting Service*. Viking.

Robinson, Barbara. *The Best Christmas Pageant Ever*. Avon/Camelot.

Roddy, Lee. *The Overland Escape*. Bethany House. (also other titles in his American Adventure series)

Selden, George. *The Cricket in Times Square*. Dell.

Smith, Robert Kimmel. *Chocolate Fever*. Dell.

Thomsen, Paul. *Mountain of Fire*. Wolgemuth & Hyatt. (also other titles in the Creation Adventure series)

Warner, Gertrude Chandler. *The Boxcar Children*. Whitman.

White, E. B. *Charlotte's Web*. Harper & Row.

Wilder, Laura Ingalls. *Little House on the Prairie*. Harper & Row.

Note: A number of Christian biographies are available from the following publishers:
> Bethany House Publishers
> Moody Press
> Mott Media
> Wolgemuth & Hyatt

Other Resources

Trelease, Jim. *The Read-Aloud Handbook*. Penguin Press.

Hunt, Gladys. *Honey for a Child's Heart*. Zondervan.

McEwan, Elaine K. *How to Raise a Reader*. David C. Cook

Your Christian bookstore manager.

◊ Appendix E ◊

Travel Supplies

Choose from the list below some items you think your children would enjoy taking along when traveling:

Markers
Coloring books (pictures, abstract designs)
"Yes and Know" books with invisible markers
Card games
Bible games
Ungame (board not needed, just use cards)
Viewmasters
Fun pads
Pocket trivia games
Magnetic chess, checkers, etc.
Rubik's Cube
Car Bingo
Books
Kaleidoscope
Pencils and paper
Stencils
Play on Words (Milton Bradley)
Merlin (Parker Brothers)
Pocket Pictures (A form of Pictionary)
Speak and Spell
Spell and Math

Magazines
Cassette tapes
Plenty of batteries

Recommended Resources for Family Travelers:

Games to Play in the Car, by Michael Harwood, Congdon and Weed, 1967, 1983.

Family Car Songbook, Running Press, 1983.

How to Take Great Trips With Your Kids, by Sanford and Joan Portnoy, Harvard Common Press, 1983.

Best Travel Activity Book Ever, Rand McNally (games, puzzles, riddles, etc.).

Are We There Yet?, Rand McNally.

◇ Appendix F ◇

Resources for Family Spiritual Nutrition

Memorization Tools

The Navigators publish the "Topical Memory System" for adults, using small cards with verses printed on them and another system for children, called "Well-Versed Kids." People are encouraged to work at their own pace on these verses that center around salvation and Christian growth topics. "Well-Versed Kids" comes with a parent-teacher manual to clarify some of the spiritual concepts taught in the verses. Both of these Navigators materials are available through Christian bookstores or from NavPress. (See below for address.)

Bible Memory Association also has separate children and adult programs as well as a family plan, in which all the members of the family memorize essentially the same material. Adults memorize more verses each week than children, and older kids memorize more than younger ones. The verses are printed in pocket- or purse-size booklets along with a brief, age-appropriate commentary or explanation. A reasonable enrollment fee helps defray expenses and covers the cost of rewards given upon completion of the memory work. Rewards consist of such things as Christian books and games, Bibles, and plaques. (See below for address.)

Addresses for Memorization and Devotional Material Resources

The Bible League, 16801 Van Dam Rd., South Holland, IL 60473. Phone: (312) 331–2094.

Bible Memory Association, Box 12000, Ringgold, LA 71068–2000.

The Family Altar, Back to God Hour, 6555 West College Dr., Palos Heights, IL 60463. Phone: (312) 371–8700.

Family Walk, Walk Through the Bible, P.O. Box 476, Mt. Morris, IL 61054.

Keys for Kids, Box 1, Grand Rapids, MI 49506.

The Navigators, P.O. Box 6000, Colorado Springs, CO 80934.

Wycliffe Bible Translators (send for name of a tribe without translators—for which to pray), P.O. Box 2727, Huntington Beach, CA 92647. Phone: (714) 536–9346.

Devotional Aids for Kids and Families

The Christian Family Bedtime Reading Book, edited by Ron and Lyn Klug. Augsburg Publishing House. A collection of stories, poems, prayers, and lullabies—some about common childhood experiences and some to help children overcome their fears. For primary and middle grades.

Every Day With God, published by Word Publishing. Based on the *International Children's Bible*, this book has 52 five-days-per week sections, each two pages long. A day's reading includes pictures, a Scripture passage, memory verse, and prayer. For children 7–10.

Little Visits With God, by Allan Hart Jahsmann and Martin P. Simon. Concordia Publishing House. This classic includes a Bible story, questions to discuss, a suggested Bible passage, and a brief prayer. Especially appropriate for younger grade-school children.

Mark: God on the Move, by Carolyn Nystrom. Harold Shaw Publishers. A 16-lesson inductive Bible study with an introductory paragraph and questions with blanks for each lesson. Part of the Young Fisherman Bible Study Guide series. Appropriate for junior high and for some students in middle grades.

My Father's World, by Joanne E. De Jonge. Board of Publications of the Christian Reformed Church. Series of four books celebrating creation as God's world. Each book is a collection of 23 essays.

Includes *The Rustling Grass* about plants, *All Nature Sings* about insects and small animals, *Of Skies and Seas* about birds and sea creatures, and *My Listening Ears* about the human body. Ages 6–13.

My Magnificent Machine, by William L. Coleman. Bethany House Publishers. Fifty-two brief, warm devotionals about the marvels of the human body. For primary and middle grades. There are many other Coleman devotional titles available from Bethany.

The NIV Serendipity Bible for Study Groups, published by Zondervan Publishing Company. Contains the complete NIV Bible with three kinds of questions in the margins: questions to get ready for Bible study, questions to dig into the Scriptures, and questions to apply the Scriptures to life. Appropriate for middle and upper grades.

No Kidding, God, by James C. Schaap. CRC Publications. Sixty devotionals based on the Psalms. Well-written, real-life material, each devotional includes a suggested Bible passage, a meditation, and closing prayer. Also in the series is *Someone's Singing, Lord*, based on well-known hymns. Designed for middle-school children, but suitable for younger and older ones as well.

The One-year Book of Family Devotions, published by Tyndale House Publishers. Collection of 365 family devotions taken from issues of *Keys for Kids*. Each day's devotions include a Scripture reading, motto, questions, and verse to memorize. Two volumes available, appropriate for primary and middle grades.

Secrets of the Best Choice, by Lois Walfrid Johnson. NavPress. Thirty short, open-ended stories to provoke thought and encourage discussion with parents about choices and values, covering such topics as quitters, fear, self-esteem, and bullies. (See also other titles in the Let's-Talk-About-It series: *You're Worth More Than You Think!*, *Thanks for Being My Friend*, *You Are Wonderfully Made!*)

Stretch, published by Tyndale House Publishers. One year's worth of Scripture reading in bite-sized pieces—one page per day. This book selects passages from throughout the Bible to provide an overview of it. Includes pictures and space to record responses to what is read. Appropriate for middle and upper grades.

Stuck Like Glue, by Paula Rinehart. NavPress. This workbook lets the Bible speak about friends and friendships. Includes stickers to be attached to pages and space to answer questions. Other books in the series include *One of a Kind* and *Never Too Small for God*. For middle and upper grades. Could be used alone or for group discussions.

365 Bible Stories for Children, by Melanie Burnette. David C. Cook. One Bible story for each day of the year, covering the whole scope of the Bible. A spiral-bound flip book that can lie open to the day's Bible story, this book can be read alone by children eight and up, and can be read to children four and up.

Notes

Chapter One

1. M. Scott Peck, *The Road Less Traveled* (New York: Simon & Schuster, 1978), p. 15.
2. Maxine Hancock, *Creative, Confident Children* (Old Tappan, N.J.: Revell, 1985), p. 13.
3. Dr. Haim Ginott, *Between Parent and Child* (New York: Avon Books, 1965), p. 107.
4. Bruno Bettelheim, *A Good Enough Parent* (New York: A.A. Knopf, 1987), p. 16
5. Dolores Curran, *Traits of a Healthy Family* (New York: Ballantine Books, 1984), p. vi.
6. Anne Ortland, *Children Are Wet Cement* (Old Tappan, N.J.: Revell, 1981), p. 49.

Chapter Two

1. Gigi Graham Tchividjian, *Christian Parenting*, July/August 1990, p. 72.
2. Perry L. Draper, *Parents, Take Charge* (Wheaton, Ill.: Tyndale House Publishers, 1982), p. 36.

Chapter Three

1. Dr. Don Dinkmeyer and Dr. Gary D. McKay, *Raising a Responsible Child* (New York: Simon & Schuster, 1973), p. 166.
2. Joyce Milburn, *Helping Your Children Love Each Other* (Minneapolis, Minn.: Bethany House Publishers, 1983), p. 33.
3. Bruce Narramore, *Help! I'm a Parent* (Grand Rapids, Mich.: Zondervan Publishers, 1972), p. 162.
4. Verna Birkey and Jeanette Turnquist, *A Mother's Problem Solver* (Old Tappan, N.J.: Revell, 1978), p. 15.

Chapter Four

1. Verna Birkey and Jeanette Turnquist, *A Mother's Problem Solver* (Old Tappan, N.J.: Revell, 1978), p. 35.

Chapter Five

1. Louis and Kay Moore, *When You Both Go to Work: How Two-Paycheck Families Can Stay Alive in the Church* (Waco, Tex.: Word, Inc., 1982), p. 147.
2. Mary Beth Moster, *When Mom Goes to Work* (Chicago, Ill.: Moody Press, 1980), pp. 60–61.
3. Jayne Garrison, *The Christian Working Mother's Handbook* (Wheaton, Ill.: Tyndale House Publishers, 1986), p. 51.
4. Ibid., pp. 177–178.
5. Dr. Pat Finn, "Children in a Two Briefcase Family," *Family Life Today*, November 1985, p. 19.
6. Dorothy Glasser Weiss, "Good Mothers Don't Get Mad and Other Myths of Parenting," *Child*, January-February 1990, pp. 97–98.
7. Ibid.

Chapter Six

1. Dr. Ashley Montagu quoted in "How to Raise a Civilized Child," by Eleanor Berman, *Working Mother*, January 1989, p. 82.
2. Ibid.
3. Sharon Sheppard, "How to Foster Creativity in Children," *The Standard*, July 1987, p. 32.
4. From "Choosing Children's Books" in *Parents and Children* (Wheaton, Ill.: Victor Books, 1986), p. 274.

5. "What Would We Do Without Art?" by Lisa Livingston, *Moody Monthly*, December 1984, p. 26.
6. Dean and Grace Merrill, *Together at Home* (Nashville, Tenn.: Thomas Nelson Publishers, 1985), p. 9.
7. Howard Hendricks, "Can TV Be Effective for Education?" in *Parents and Children* (Wheaton, Ill.: Victor Books, 1986), p. 275.
8. Jerry Jenkins, "TV: An Epitaph for Values," *Moody Monthly*, April 1988, p. 6.
9. Noel Holston, "Folks in Sitcoms Live Beyond Means," *Minneapolis Star Tribune*, January 6, 1991, p. 1F.
10. Jenkins, p. 6.
11. Judy David, Ed.D., "TV: When to Turn It On—and Off," *Good Housekeeping*, September 1988, p. 154.
12. Quoted in "Can TV Be Effective for Education?" by Howard Hendricks in *Parents and Children* (Wheaton, Ill.: Victor Books, 1986), p. 275.

Chapter Seven

1. Verna Birkey and Jeanette Turnquist, *Building Happy Memories and Family Traditions* (Old Tappan, N.J.: Revell, 1980), p. 59.

Chapter Eight

1. Personal interview by Joyce K. Ellis with Paul Little, June 25, 1975.
2. Andrew Murray, *The Believer's Daily Renewal* (Minneapolis, Minn.: Bethany House Publishers, 1981), p. 16.
3. Ibid.
4. Ibid, p. 17.
5. Jayne Garrison, *The Christian Working Mother's Handbook* (Wheaton, Ill.: Tyndale House Publishers, 1986), pp. 103–104.

Chapter Nine

1. Dean and Grace Merrill, *Together at Home* (Nashville, Tenn.: Thomas Nelson Publishers, 1985), pp. 9–10.
2. Harold J. Sala, *How to Enjoy Raising Your Children* (Denver, Colo.: Accent Books, 1984), p. 152.
3. Mary White, *Successful Family Devotions* (Colorado Springs, Colo.: NavPress, 1981), cover.
4. Ibid, pp. 140–141.

5. Ibid, p. 12.
6. Merrill, pp. 60–61.
7. Ibid.

Chapter Ten

1. Dan Kiley, *Dr. Dan's Prescriptions: 1001 Nonmedical Hints for Solving Parenting Problems* (New York, N.Y.: Coward, McCann and Geoghegan, 1982), p. 236.
2. Melissa Bregenzer, "Mommy, I'm Bored," *Ladies' Home Journal,* July 1990, p. 78.
3. Howard Hendricks, "Your Child Needs Unstructured Time," *Parents and Children* (Wheaton, Ill.: Victor Books, 1986), p. 269.

Chapter Eleven

1. Dianne Hales and Robert E. Hales, M.D., "Babes in Stressland," *American Health,* October 1989, p. 45.
2. Carole K. Halmrast, "Why We Aren't Going for the Gold," *McCalls,* July 1984, p. 154.
3. Ibid.

Chapter Twelve

1. T. Berry Brazelton, M.D., *Working and Caring* (Reading, Mass.: Addison Wesley, 1985), p. 181.
2. Ibid.
3. Verna Birkey and Jeanette Turnquist, *Building Happy Memories and Family Traditions* (Old Tappan, N.J.: Revell, 1980), p. 9.
4. Alice Fulton and Pauline Hatch, *It's Here . . . Somewhere* (Cincinnati: Writer's Digest Books, 1985), p. 25.
5. Dolores Curran, *Traits of a Healthy Family* (New York: Ballantine Books, 1984), p. 226.
6. Anthony Campolo, *Who Switched the Price Tags?* (Waco, Tex.: Word, 1986), p. 135.
7. Ibid, pp. 136–137.
8. Bettelheim as quoted by Harold B. Smith in "Superkids and Superparents," *Christianity Today,* Sept. 18, 1987, p. 15.